INTO-ME-SEE

Mom Mary
The Best!

Dr. Jeannette

INTO-ME-SEE

MASTERING

BLACK INTIMACY

FOR THE

RELATIONSHIP

YOU'VE ALWAYS

WANTED

DR. JEANNELLE PERKINS-MUHAMMAD, LMFT

RIVER GROVE
BOOKS

This book is intended as a reference volume only. It is sold with the understanding that the publisher and author are not engaged in rendering any professional services. The information given here is designed to help you make informed decisions. If you suspect that you have a problem that might require professional treatment or advice, you should seek competent help.

Published by River Grove Books
Austin, TX
www.rivergrovebooks.com

Distributed by River Grove Books

Design and composition by Greenleaf Book Group and Sheila Parr
Cover design by Greenleaf Book Group and Sheila Parr
Cover image used under license from ©istock.com/PeopleImages
Image used under license from ©Shutterstock/Patricia Soon
Images of brain and words of love ©Shutterstock/1902849208
©Shutterstock/ 242127580

Publisher's Cataloging-in-Publication data is available.

Print ISBN: 978-1-63299-650-3

eBook ISBN: 978-1-63299-651-0

First Edition

Whenever I feel weak, I remember those who make me strong. Moreover, whenever I start to doubt myself, I remember those who believe in me. When I am strong, I give to those around me who are weak, because I believe in them.

I dedicate this work to my kids, Quortney and Nyjai—"I got two of them."

To Claudette, Cokeitha, Darice, Doris, John, Jeff, Karen, Lakisha, Pat, Sam, Teruko, Thoressa, and my "village" for making me laugh and allowing me to be vulnerable.

A very specific dedication goes to my parents and grandparents, who taught me the value of authenticity, family, faith, and fastidious devotion. I never would have made it without you!

I want to acknowledge my editors, creative team,
and publisher for their excellence.

Contents

The Courage of Into-Me-See

B y the time that Raymond and Rachel came to see me, they had been married for 17 years and together for more than 20 years. Raymond was in his mid-40s; Rachel had just celebrated her 40th birthday. Over the past few years, Raymond had had several affairs with multiple woman yet often told Rachel that her intuition about him cheating was wrong. She decided to begin searching his phone and social media accounts and found more than she thought was possible. Rachel said that she loves her husband and was very hurt.

But when it could no longer be denied that Raymond was cheating, they both recognized that either they needed to work on their relationship or they needed to call it quits. If I told you they ended up divorced, you wouldn't be surprised, would you? But that's not what happened. The couple agreed to rebuild trust and develop deeper intimacy through marriage counseling.

You can probably predict what I heard in the first session with them. Raymond said that all Rachel did was complain.

"She's not giving me enough sex! What's a man supposed to do?" he said. Rachel told me that Raymond was not affectionate. "We don't spend enough time together. I never see him. He's not helping with the kids or doing anything around the house. All he ever wants to do is 'tap that ass.'"

There were many factors at work for this couple. In counseling they realized that external influences such as family, work, friends, sports, hobbies, and trekking children around were impeding their ability to connect. It turned out that despite having been together for two decades, neither knew the other very well. Both were dealing with anxiety and depression, only some of which could be attributed to the pandemic. Raymond had suffered through many adverse childhood experiences and trauma that were still affecting his adult behavior. Rachel felt Raymond was not emotionally expressive or supportive. She had grown up longing for her father's attention and transferred that energy to Raymond.

They came to understand that their primary **love languages**—how they received and expressed love—were different. Raymond's was physical touch, including, but not limited to, having sex. Which makes his complaint "she's not giving me enough sex!" perfectly understandable. Rachel's primary love language was acts of service: doing nice things for one another. Thus, "he's not doing anything around the house" diminished her affection toward him. Both had a shared love language of quality time, wanting to spend more time together with just the two of them.

What brought this couple back from the brink of divorce was their courage and commitment to truly open themselves to each other. The work they did together wasn't complicated, but it was difficult at times—particularly for Raymond, who had to make enormous changes fast in order to earn Rachel's trust. They learned how to open up to each other using a format they both found challenging: starting with an "I feel" statement about one particular topic, then talking about why the feeling exists, followed by an "I need" statement to assist in finding a compromise. This structured format for discussions was very foreign to them since they stated, "We generally don't talk like this in our animated debates," which tended to involve raised voices or yelling arguments cloaked in passionate discussions.

Today, Raymond and Rachel are more committed to staying together than ever before. They communicate more easily about everything from the mundane (calling to let the other know "I just left work and will be home in 10 minutes") to the profound (the kind of relationship with God they want their children to have). And as a result, they feel more connected to each other and both have made changes to meet the other's needs. Now, Raymond is sexually fulfilled and vulnerable with Rachel. Rachel desires Raymond because she can see his heart and experience his kindness.

THE POWER OF INTIMACY

What Raymond and Rachel did was to practice intimacy, exploring ways to deepen the depth of their connection at multiple levels: physical, mental, emotional, and spiritual. In one session, for example, they established that their spiritual communities sought to keep marriages together through prayer, unconditional love, provision, respect, and sex. Rachel said that she was constantly told that if she prayed about her husband's infidelity, the Lord would deliver him. Raymond said he knew this was true and wanted to change, but he did not feel Rachel respected him. They were caught up in the constant rumbling conversations of irritation and blame that we all know as nagging. No one in their communities discussed how to build a relationship by focusing on developing communication and intimacy skills that incorporated a mind, body, and soul connection. Nor were any of them exposed to deciphering what the expectations were for their relationship around their faiths' ideals.

Intimacy is fundamental to support and sustain a healthy romantic relationship. It illuminates the quality of a relationship and the level of satisfaction the partners enjoy. It creates much deeper, rewarding connections and a lot more of what I call HBNS (Hot Butt Naked Sex)!

In successful intimate relationships, partners are able to achieve their shared vision for their individual lives and for their relationship. They can discuss various emotions and past hurts freely, which is an indication of emotional security. Emotional security is the gateway to building healthy, deeply connected intimate relationships. The key to emotional security in a relationship is safety, knowing that your sharing will be free from judgment, having your partner validate rather than ridicule your feelings.

Yet many couples—regardless of socio-economic level, physical health, beliefs and values or family configuration—lament the lack of intimacy in their relationships. When partners discuss intimacy, it is easy to see that they have varying definitions of what it looks like and how it feels. They also have varying expectations for who initiates intimacy and the effort that should be expended to satisfy the intimacy need. Most couples think of intimacy as the sex act or what leads up to it. I hope to reframe that perspective and offer new ideas about how powerful sex can be when you understand a true intimate connection needs to involve our brain, emotions, body, and spirit.

What I work to help my clients appreciate is that differences in expectations and behaviors result from experiences and core beliefs and values rooted in their individual cultural and familial reality. "Meeting expectations" means that romantic partners want to experience connections without having to coerce or persuade. They have a desire for honest expressions of love. Authenticity—acting in ways that are true reflections of our personality and beliefs—and trust are vital to the realization of expectations, allowing romantic partners the ability to willingly open their whole being to intimacy.

To be honest, authentic, and trustworthy is to know thyself fully. This might be the first challenge for the individuals in the relationship. Once each individual acknowledges their own expectations and understands that their partner is likely thinking about intimacy differently than they are, the opportunity for change increases exponentially. At that moment, you realize it is possible to create environments that will encourage the growth of genuine and rewarding intimacy. This is your opportunity to reframe the narrative you have in your mind about how your relationships *should* work into a more positive narrative about how they *could* work. It is your opportunity to change the legacy of your relationship for generations to come. As a couple, you become more powerful in that moment.

THE ESSENCE OF INTIMACY

There are three undeniable aspects of healthy relationships: honesty, generosity, and awareness. There is a chain reaction at work here. Honesty in intimacy takes vulnerability, which in turn increases with emotional security (when your partner recognizes and prioritizes your emotions as valid and important). A partner's presence of mind to be generous with providing space for understanding and connecting with what you feel and how those feelings impact your actions requires self-awareness (the partner's recognition of their own feelings) and authenticity (actions grounded in those feelings).

Unfortunately, self-awareness is not as easily achieved as you might think. We often have subconscious barriers based on deep-rooted beliefs and values that are no longer relevant to the individual or to the relationship, and that prevents us from knowing our true minds. This lack of self-awareness leaves couples looking at one another and saying, "Becoming intimate should just take common sense." *Au contraire!* Common sense is what is common to a man's or woman's experience. Whatever you were taught, either directly or indirectly, is what common sense is for you. What you consider common sense will differ from what your partner thinks is common sense. I know some will rebuff that statement, but stick with me. I will show you what I mean.

In the places where I work and live, we often use the phrase **Into-Me-See** to describe this process. It is the ability to look past the exterior, physical attraction to your partner to see the vulnerability and needs that ooze from their pores and seek your attention. It is a commitment to share personal information about feelings and emotions that allows other people to "see into" you and for us to "see into" them. Into-Me-See is a round-about in which two people commit to providing a safe space where their greatest fears and deepest wounds can be revealed and healed in the sharing of their unique intimate expression. Such connections and exchanges allow them to realize how we relate to one another and experience the wonders of being together. In doing so, we do not accommodate the fear or shame of our past.

Fear, shame, and guilt often restrict us from allowing our partners to experience our true authentic nature. In contrast, Into-Me-See takes advantage of being authentic and allows us to experience true growth in our connection with our partners. It is in this place of Into-Me-See that regrets can be expressed, hopes revealed, loneliness soothed, and peace massaged into the fabric of the relationship. It is then that we can also understand and nurture a renewed, shared vision of intimacy, a vision that exists to benefit the couple.

Subsequently, with the shared knowledge and vision we have, we will see how intimacy leads to increased and improved health, lifestyle, and relationship satisfaction. That quality of intimacy only comes with understanding the intricacies and interconnectedness of four levels of intimacy—cognitive, emo-tional, spiritual, and physical—which you'll read about in a later chapter. Including and practicing these aspects of intimacy by sharing your vulnerability with your partner (and vice versa) can promote immense growth; wielding them as weapons can hinder romantic intimate expressions and lead to the death of a relationship.

Historically, we in the Black community have not practiced mental, emotional, or sexual wellness in relationships.[1] The
damage can be reversed with energy and effort. It is essential
to recognize our history individually and collectively as partners and acknowledge how that history impacts our mental and
emotional health. Diving deep into intimacy means accepting
that we can change what we have into what we want, if we do
the work. This work must be accomplished together. No one
partner can build an intimate relationship in a vacuum.

Black-couple intimacy surpasses the need to have sex, pro-
create, pay bills, have a physical companion, and apply for a
mortgage. Intimacy is deeply rooted in self-awareness, self-acceptance, and self-love. I mean, how can you truly love another
without knowing yourself, accepting yourself, or loving yourself first? Intimacy is directly connected to Into-Me-See. Look
beyond what you think you see and get to know the authentic
me. The authentic me must show up, though. I mean, this level
of intimacy involves openness, honesty, generosity, and vulnerability as well as an awareness of what it is to be a couple. It is the
kind of intimacy understood through the lens of social observation and exchange of information.

Intimacy is a journey of experiencing the wonders of your
partner as revealed through the **intentional and reciprocal**
exchange of unique intimate expressions. "Intentional" meaning
we should be making conscious choices about how we interact
with our partner; "reciprocal" because there must be equal give-
and-take in order for an intimate relationship to thrive.

---

1   Apryl A. Alexander, "Sex for All: Sex Positivity and Intersectionality in Clinical
     and Counseling Psychology," *Journal of Black Sexuality and Relationships* 6, no. 1
     (Summer 2019): 49-72, https://doi:10.1353/bsr.2019.0015.

This journey of authenticity and vulnerability fosters a foundational environment for an intimate revelation of what happens in your exchange. So, this ain't yo' mama and daddy's relationship. No. No. This is about baring your soul, so you get the best out of every moment, even the hard ones.

USING THIS BOOK

The purpose of this book is to help Black couples learn how to have a healthy intimate relationship that leaves a positive legacy for future generations. It promises to revolutionize how our families manifest the ability to see beyond the external and recognize our divine purpose throughout our culture. Intimacy is the energy for our very existence. As I have said many times to clients, the greatest generational wealth we can bestow to our legacy is mental and emotional wellness. Intimacy is wellness personified. That wellness has the potential to enlarge our tents as our hearts and homes swell with intimate expressions that reveal our truest power: Black love.

In this book, you will explore the ways that your personal experiences and cultural history have shaped your beliefs about intimacy and sex. You will develop a fuller understanding of what intimacy means and the work it takes to establish and maintain true intimacy with your partner. You will see how important it is to acknowledge and address mental health challenges that trap us in unhealthy thinking that leads to abnormal and destructive behaviors.

Later chapters in this book will help you do an introspective assessment so you can become more aware of what is setting your expectations and driving your own behaviors regarding

intimacy. That self-awareness is necessary to fully reciprocate
Into-Me-See as you interact with your spouse or partner in ways
that are honest and authentic to you both.

I will be challenging you to get deeply philosophical, and I
will use information and data that might stir the pot a bit. I ain't
scared to say I believe that we fail because we don't look at the
individual and communal challenges that hinder our intimate
expressions. And that is exactly why I wrote this book—to create
an opportunity to open the doors to building and sustaining intimacy within Black-couple relationships. It was written bearing
both Black males and females in mind. This is not an act of gender
profiling; it is targeted at helping us see ourselves to understand
ourselves enough to want to allow our partners to connect with
the reality of who we can be as a couple. This book is about manifestation, about making sure that we live our lives every day in
ways that are consistent with our values, hopes, and goals.

With this book, Black couples can learn to appreciate
their vulnerability, the art of reciprocating affection, and how
to connect in relationships, making them feel less like business
transactions and more like interconnections of tenderness that
build strong relational patterns of devotion. You will learn how
to attend to your own emotional needs and understand true
individual self-intimacy. You will encounter recommendations
for how to transfer and engage in authentic, honest, and trustworthy intimacy with your partner.

CHAPTER 1

What Is Intimacy?

There are years that ask questions and years that answer.
—Zora Neale Hurston

Often, men believe that sex is the most definitive way to be intimate with their partners. There is a biological problem with this thought process. The actual sex act that ends in orgasm decreases their testosterone and leaves them vulnerable emotionally. If the man has a great emotional connection with the woman he is with, this is a wonderful time to increase intimacy by talking and sharing ideas. But usually there ain't much talking happening after sex because you are both too exhausted to talk while trying to catch your breath. Not to mention, if each has a sufficiently satisfying orgasm a heavy spirit of sleepiness falls upon them.

In contrast, most women enter the relationship working to

establish a seamless flow of verbal communication with their partner. Women release tremendous amounts of oxytocin during orgasm. This creates a loving and bonding feeling that allows the woman to treasure the moment.

If the couple has a connection already, a positive sexual experience for both parties gets them well on their way to establishing trust and genuine desire for each other. Yet, even if they connect through verbal communication and sexual acts, they might find themselves able to meet only a portion of their intimacy needs. Their remaining desires require deeper knowledge of both themselves and others.

What about you? When you hear the word "intimacy," do you think first about physical or sexual intimacy? If you said yes, you're not alone. But there is much more to intimacy than the physical.

Take Shareta and Samuel, for example. They are a couple in their 50s who have been together more than 30 years. They have four children and one grandchild. Shareta admitted in our sessions to having feelings of anxiety about sex. Samuel described how he was still dealing with the loss of his father some years ago and the more recent passing of his mother. This grief created a mild depressive state of mind. Also, Covid-19 affected the dynamics of their relationship, and during the pandemic they found themselves struggling to connect.

Shareta was physically and mentally tired from her commitments to work and to her family. She said that Samuel got on her nerves because he was too demanding. He constantly tapped her on the butt, showed up in her doorway naked, and made passes during the most inopportune moments. Now that she

was in her fifties, sex had become painful for her and she said
Samuel was not gentle. As a result, the couple had sex only twice
a year. This did not sit well for Samuel.

But the lack of sexual intimacy was only one factor in the
downswing of their relationship; other factors were at work.
For example, what had started out as teasingly affectionate
comments in the early years of their marriage had turned into
mean-spirited, hurtful jokes.

Samuel framed their goals this way: "We don't want to
divorce. We want to improve our marriage and our love life. I
hope we can rekindle the romance and speak to each other in a
more soothing manner."

For Shareta and Samuel, like most couples, becoming more
intimate involved working on multiple issues, not just sex. They
were aging and the demands on their lives were changing.
Shareta was going through menopause and Samuel was concerned that he was less attractive to her since he gained weight.
They agreed they had become more irritable and cantankerous
with everything except the children. This meant they needed
to re-evaluate their beliefs and values, hopes and dreams, and
goals for the future. This required them to think beyond the sex,
though technically, that was their immediate goal.

There are, in fact, four levels of intimacy important to all
couples: cognitive, emotional, physical, and spiritual. Couples
need to operate at all four levels to achieve true intimacy, and
how these levels do or do not interact can promote or hinder
a romantic relationship. As preparation for understanding how
to create a deeper intimacy between you and your partner, let's
explore each of these levels.

COGNITIVE INTIMACY

Cognitive intimacy is all about how we connect to one another based on our intellect. It occurs when couples exchange thoughts and share ideas.[2] Cognitive intimacy is the result of couples engaging in effective and honest communication. Healthy communication requires partners to define and clarify ideals, perspectives, and paradigms of thought in this exchange. Intellectual compatibility is vital to cognitive intimacy. Cognitive intimacy is usually expressed through discussion about the thoughts, beliefs, goals, and displays of vulnerability that create experiences and understanding within the relationship. It creates nurturing fibers that provide the foundation for all intimacy.

This cognitive connection often occurs in the dating phase of a relationship. There may be opportunities to discuss childhood experiences, both positive and negative, including everything from success in a school play or interactions with the neighborhood bully to extracurricular activities or the lack of emotional vulnerability, food, or safety that existed in your home. You might discuss politics, sexuality, or even your perspective on social norms past, current, and future. These conversations open the bowels of vulnerability to validate feelings of anger, loneliness, or the strength and tenacity of the family. You might have felt loved and adored or grateful to have extended family that cared for you while your mom worked two jobs, for example. This adoration for family could have created a value system that impacts your relationship (for example, having extended family visiting every weekend is a positive expression of love).

---

2   Rosemary Blieszner and Brian De Vries, "Introduction: Perspectives on Intimacy," *Generations* 25 no. 2 (Summer 2001): 7-8.

Through these cognitively intimate moments you come to understand how your partner came to their worldview on childrearing, politics, spending, gender roles, and maybe spousal responsibilities. Your efforts to discuss these matters can often evolve into a stream of consciousness that allows you both an opportunity for Into-Me-See. Remember Into-Me-See is the ability to look past the exterior, physical attraction of your partner and see the vulnerability and needs that ooze from their pores and seek your attention. It is a commitment to share personal information about feelings and emotions that allows other people to "see into" you and for you to "see into" them.

Cognitive intimacy can create a feeling of safety between a couple. The concept of reciprocity is key here: this kind of deeper connection necessitates that each partner match the level of vulnerability being expressed by the other. There is no room to judge, scowl at, or dismiss an experience shared by the other person. Even poking fun at or laughing at an experience your partner does not find funny could derail efforts to create safety through cognitive intimacy. The more you reciprocate through healthy, emotionally safe, positive, and effective communication, the more fondness and closeness you can build within your relationship. This practice of **relational reciprocity**—partners exchanging their innermost thoughts equally—establishes the foundation for emotional, spiritual, and sexual intimacy.

Improving Cognitive Intimacy

One of the best examples of improving cognitive intimacy comes from the story of Raymond and Rachel, the couple I described in the introduction. One of the simplest but most powerful steps they took was to spend 15 to 30 minutes a day *with each other.* No electronics. No TV. They called it "tea time" (though other beverages were often involved!). Tea time was scheduled for when the kids were either in bed or out of the house for some activity.

The only rule during tea time was that Raymond and Rachel *could talk about anything EXCEPT problems.* That meant they ended up sharing thoughts and ideas on everything from what was going on in the world to their personal histories and experiences. They came to truly know one another like never before. They began to be vulnerable about recent fears and challenges about what it meant to be Black in America, the changes they were seeing in their bodies and what they were told about getting older, the things they missed about childhood, and the impact of not living closer to family.

I highly recommend this tea time approach, but also encourage you to look for other ways to simply talk with your partner and exchange thoughts and ideas. There are many games available online.

EMOTIONAL INTIMACY

Love recognizes no barriers. It jumps hurdles, leaps fences, penetrates walls to arrive at its destination full of hope.

—Maya Angelou

Emotional intimacy is experienced in the exchange of feelings between one person and another. And these feelings are generally deeply rooted in the value of self-disclosure, having the courage to talk about your own ideas and reactions. True emotional intimacy encompasses the full range of emotions that we humans can experience. Brené Brown, a human behavior researcher, completed a study of the number of emotions experienced by its participants. Of the 7,000 surveyed, the majority were able to name three emotions readily: happiness, sadness, and anger.

You might think that is a small number as you consider what you have felt reading the first couple of pages of this book. In actuality, it makes sense that we are limited in our emotional expression because our vocabulary for emotional language is bound by the experiences within the culture in which we grew up. Not to mention, many of the emotions we felt as children were dismissed and ridiculed. The shame those feelings instilled was never to be felt again.

So one of the first steps in developing deeper emotional intimacy is to acknowledge and accept the fuller range of emotions that we all experience as humans. Table 1 shows a table that my colleagues and I use to help partners explore emotions beyond love and hate. You can find a copy of this table in Appendix A (Tools).

Sad	Happy	Hurt	Helped	Insecure	Confident	Tired	Energized
Depressed	Hopeful	Abused	Cherished	Weak	Strong	Indifferent	Determined
Lonely	Supported	Forgotten	Befriended	Hopeless	Brave	Bored	Inspired
Disgusted	Charmed	Ignored	Appreci-ated	Doubtful	Certain	Drained	Creative
Angry	Grateful	Judged	Understood	Scared	Assured	Sick	Healthy
Frustrated	Calm	Offended	Commend-ed	Anxious	Prepared	Exhausted	Renewed
Annoyed	Amused	Victimized	Empowered	Defeated	Successful	Dull	Vibrant
Discour-aged	Optimistic	Rejected	Accepted	Worthless	Valuable	Weary	Alert
Upset	Content	Cursed	Blessed	Guilty	Forgiven	Paralyzed	Enlivened
Despairing	Joyful	Destroyed	Healed	Ugly	Beautify	Powerless	Strength-ened
Uninter-ested	Enthusi-astic	Hated	Loved	Pressured	At ease	Dejected	Motivated
Disap-pointed	Thrilled	Despised	Esteemed	Forced	Encour-aged	Listless	Focused
Hateful	Loving	Mistreated	Taken care of	Stressed	Peaceful	Burned-out	Rejuve-nated
Bitter	Kind	Crushed	Reassured	Nervous	Relaxed	Fatigued	Invigorated
Sorrowful	Celebratory	Injured	Made whole	Worried	Secure	Blah	Animated
Mournful	Overjoyed	Tortured	Saved	Embar-rassed	Comforted	Stale	Refreshed

Table 1: Feelings

Emotional intimacy is a complex issue not just because we have so many emotions, but because they are based on many factors:

- What memories and experiences we store in our brains;
- Our brain's interpretation of those memories and experiences (how we make meaning out of the experiences);
- Our feelings (love, shame, pride, etc.);
- How we work out conflicting or incongruent thoughts and reach decisions;
- How our senses interpret stimuli from the outside world (sounds, smells, sight, taste, touch).

Because of these factors, two people who share the exact same experience can feel differently about the experience overall.

When we are transparent and forthcoming with our feelings, we want our partners to understand them, embrace them, validate them, and also reciprocate the level of transparency and energy in their expression of feelings toward us. As sharers and receivers, we can perform these roles when we have learned the skills required to do intimacy better. The skills require attentiveness and commitment to a shared vision. Here, we listen to learn and understand; we look to see and comprehend. We do this because we want to understand our needs and the needs of our partner. When we understand what these needs are, we can deliver them in the most efficient ways.

Even those married for 20, 30, or 40 years, and seemingly embodying an ideal marriage, aren't having a party every day of their union. They are also facing challenges in their marriage, but their ability to look past these challenges to see the bigger picture is significant. They may have learned to be more resilient and open to new experiences over the years, granting each permission to change. If we pay attention to our relationships, we will identify the things that will most likely sabotage peace and intimacy in our relationships. These hindrances must be minimized.

Delving into emotional intimacy takes greater work than simply having a conversation about the weather or your workday. It requires that you get to know the intimate details of your partner's experiences, so you can understand the feelings they associate with their experiences and how those connect with their history. It is an emotional exploration in a safe, non-judgmental environment. The emotional connection includes intentionally, you know, actually thinking about what your partner tells you about their day and connecting it with your knowledge of them. It means that you allow their emotional state, no matter what it is, to be accepted in the space you share, without judgment. It is knowing when to problem-solve or simply listen, or, most importantly, when to express empathy for your partner's experience.

The emotional responses you will receive from or give to your partner are probably more influenced by your tone of voice than by the words you actually say. If your partner reveals a difficult experience, for example, their reaction to a response of "oh, really" will vary greatly depending on how you say that phrase. Do you sound harsh and skeptical? Understanding and accepting? Calm and inviting?

Emotional intimacy can be a terrifying space if you are not open to discovery. Insecurities can spring up in ways that sabotage connection and create competition within the relationship. When this happens, the relationship teeters on the cusp like frayed fringes. It is vital to ensure there is an opportunity to be authentic in expressing emotions. So, if you don't feel like doing something, say no. If you say yes and then behave like you're annoyed, you'll set resentment in motion.

SEXUAL INTIMACY

We all want more HBNS (which you may recall means Hot Butt Naked Sex). The pathway to HBNS is to build on cognitive and emotional intimacy and realize that sexual intimacy is just a type of physical intimacy.

"Sexual intimacy is the act of being attracted to another person and consciously choosing to share one's body with them through physical contact, affection, and sexual activities."[3] It is best experienced when emotional intimacy manifests into sexual behavior. Because it involves all those aspects of physical interaction, sex will be discussed in this book as an *experience* and not just an *act*.

There is a general belief in the Black community that women do not desire sex as much as men do. We tend to believe that women are taught to wait on men to initiate the sexual experience, so it is necessary to encourage women to desire sex as much as men do because they are free beings. We cannot encourage intimacy among couples if one-half of the couple has been cultured to believe that sex is a "man's thing." Therefore, putting this awareness here will embolden women, take the stress off

---

3   Dogan, J., Hargons, C., Meiller, C., Oluokun, J., Montique, C., & Malone, N. (2018). "Cathin' Feelings: Experiences of Intimacy during Black College Students' Sexual Encounters." *Journal of Black Sexuality and Relationships*, 5(2), 810107. https://doi. org/10.1353/bsr.2018.0021

men, and foster intimacy among couples. Because, let's be real. Women want sex and a lot of sex. However, what *we*—because I am a woman and am going to take the liberty to speak for us at this moment—truly desire is exceptionally good sex. Not the kind that makes you reach for your phone to play Candy Crush after you have cum. We want the sexual intimacy that leaves us unable to stabilize our legs or feel our feet hit the floor because the connection leaves us limp and breathless.

Seventy percent of the couples I have counseled are sexual partners, but they do not have healthy, satisfying sex with each other. There is more to sexual intimacy than simple penetration and orgasm. If penetration and orgasm were all that was needed for sexual encounter, we wouldn't bother with falling in love. The act of penetration and the sometimes orgasmic effect is the physical manifestation of the sex act. But penetration alone is a transaction, equivalent to couples discussing how to refinance car loans and mortgages or making plans for the kids. Transactional discussions in the sexual encounters between couples won't avail them any emotional bonding opportunities. Remember what I said earlier about the vulnerability that exists when men orgasm? Imagine how this time would allow for cuddling, speaking softly, enjoying sweet touches, and expressing appreciation. These are emotional and sexual exchanges that translate into deeper connections.

Now, don't get me wrong, there are those moments when you just want a quickie or are satisfying an individual need for one partner or the other. However, only six percent of women have an orgasm through penetration. So a woman may receive greater satisfaction from a conversation about refinancing the mortgage than from sex, if all you do is penetrate her.

Since couples need sexual intimacy as much as they need other aspects of intimacy, they must understand that greater frequency of sexual satisfaction will make their relationship stronger, thereby fostering healthy intimacy; unsatisfying sex or a lack of sex will hinder intimacy. I conducted a private study with couples who've come to me over the last 15 years, and it became clear that a lack of sexual satisfaction correlates with irritation, depression, anxiety, high blood pressure, infidelity, use of pornography, and immense sexual frustration. (You can find the survey in Appendix B.) Now I'm not saying there are no other factors connected to these conditions. I'm simply saying that I am seeing relationships that have low to no sexual intimacy and that most have those challenges. When we work on intimacy, I see these conditions decrease.

So, how is sexual intimacy diminished over time? The couples I talk with almost always report missed opportunities for sexual satisfaction. Table 2 illustrates how these missed opportunities can accumulate over time. And when this dissatisfaction continues, couples will perceive sexual intercourse as a duty rather than as a pleasurable experience of shared intimacy.

Years married	Avg. X sex per week	Sex per month/missed opportunities	Yr. total	Missed opportunities over time of marriage
5	3	12/8	144/96	480
10	2	8/12	96/144	1440
15	1	4/16	48/192	2880

Table 2: Missed opportunities for maximum pleasure

If couples desire to utilize every opportunity they have to experience sex, they should work to fill the gaps that exist in their sexual, emotional, spiritual, and cognitive intimacy. There will always be ebbs and flows in intimacy. That does not mean sexual intimacy has to decrease the longer you are in a relationship. You have to be intentional and focused on the ways in which you use your intimacy energy toward growing the connection.

Improving Sexual Intimacy

For Shareta and Samuel improving their sexual intimacy began by having them practice touching and speaking more gently with each other. Samuel used to smack Shareta on the bottom as he walked by. It annoyed her. Shareta thought something was wrong with her because "every woman wants a man to touch her and show interest. But it really bothers me, and I don't know why." After a number of conversations about her childhood and teen years, she revealed that as a child, she saw unwanted touching in her family that eventually turned into incest. Samuel had no idea. With that revelation, they made a cognitive connection that linked to their emotional and sexual intimacy. That might never have occurred without their having processed the family dynamic. The discussion of sexual trauma now had an opportunity to heal them and allow them to grow their intimate connection.

Next, they learned how to watch their tone of voice and learned how to be more gentle when touching each other, both during and outside of sexual intimacy. I gave Shareta several books to read about how women's bodies change as they get older and about how to make adjustments in sexual acts and positions to enhance pleasure and minimize pain or discomfort. As Shareta and Samuel became more physically and emotionally attuned to each other, they were able to return to a healthy and much more active sex life. They went from twice a year to once a week. I anticipate that as they continue to build intimacy, their frequency will increase as well. Sexual intimacy is viable as long as both partners are willing to make change.

Raymond and Rachel's situation was slightly different. Raymond was a giver in terms of sexual intimacy; he truly enjoyed pleasing Rachel. But he didn't know what she liked and enjoyed. The problem was, neither did Rachel! So their work involved experimenting with different ways to touch and connect during sex so they could discover what both partners (not just Rachel) enjoyed. They tried massage oils, whips, feathers, bondage, metal and plastic chains, hot and cold baths, remote-controlled vaginal toys, as well as simultaneously staring into each other's eyes and deep breathing. Not everything worked. Rachel and Raymond found themselves exploring kink that they had thought of a taboo because of the culture they grew up in. Now, they expressed pleasure in knowing their partner was open to new experiences. I reminded them that this was their relationship and whatever they needed to make it work was valid.

Every couple is going to be unique in terms of what it takes for them to have a fulfilling physically intimate relationship. *Don't* try to copy exactly what any other couples do, but *do* experiment to find out what works for you and your partner.

If nothing else, go back to the basics:

Practice touching each other gently. Not only with your hands, but also with other objects (e.g., paddles, flogs, feathers, chains, etc.).

- Learn to speak up about what you need and want from physical expressions of intimacy. If a particular level of pain feels good, say so.

- If physical or sexual touch is too painful or causes discomfort, find out why. Research the issue by reading books and talking to specialists. There are almost always things you can do to increase pleasure and reduce pain.

SPIRITUAL INTIMACY

Definitions and discussions of intimacy often cover only the three topics already discussed in this chapter: the cognitive, emotional, and physical closeness one experiences with a partner in a reciprocal relationship. But there is one aspect of intimacy especially important to the Black community that is too often overlooked: spirituality.

Spiritual intimacy is a phenomenon characterized by shared thoughts and feelings about religion, existentialism, and morality.[4] It is about making connections around the similarities in our beliefs and values. Some people believe that we are all spiritually connected by nature of being alive and that our spirits connect through soul ties to other realms. Spiritual intimacy requires

---

4   Dennis A. Bagarozzi, *Enhancing Intimacy in Marriage: A Clinician's Guide* (New York: Routledge, 2014).

an understanding of what was, is, and will be for a couple who desire the creation of an extraordinary, beautiful relationship. Spiritual intimacy will often exude a love that is visible between partners but should be protected from external forces.

Many Black families are religious, and a lot more believe in a collective spirituality that creates a bond between members of the family. If a Black adult who has been exposed to spirituality becomes a part of an intimacy where spirituality is *not* regarded, the disregard for religious spirituality by their partner can derail their chances at intimacy. It becomes the foundation that permeates the couples' intimate connection. Like-minded spiritual intimacy propagates genuine affection and adoration between romantic couples.

Improving Spiritual Intimacy

Both couples discussed in this chapter—Shareta and Samuel, and Raymond and Rachel—were raised in the church and had strong faith-based relationships, though they differed in their churchgoing activity. But neither had openly talked about the religious component of spiritual intimacy, nor had they talked about the way it impacted their intimate expressions. Though Raymond and Rachel were 20 years into their relationship, they had never talked about how they each wanted spirituality to be evoked in their family, nor about the lessons they wanted to impart to their children. Additionally, they dared not discuss topics they felt were forbidden because of religion. For example, were toys in the bedroom the same as cheating, or was masturbation wrong if they did it together?

Being able to talk openly about issues like these is important for Black couples. Those discussions should go beyond religious beliefs so that partners can talk about their beliefs and morals and basic philosophy of life.

Raymond and Rachel were avid church attendees. They raised their children in the ministry too. Rachel struggled with some of the ideas presented in the materials I shared with her. For example, she believed that oral sex was "only conducted between homosexual couples and an abomination to God's designed purpose in marriage." Though she had emotional needs and often felt neglected, she was always told not to share those feelings, as "it might make [her husband] seek comfort in another woman." These types of beliefs and values were eroding Rachel's connection to the relationship. They were making her resentful and sometimes "angry that [she felt she had] no power."

While some of Rachel's beliefs were religiously spiritual, others were culturally spiritual. Hmmm, culturally spiritual... You know, like when your grandmother would say, "Never let your man out of the house without emptying his balls." (Y'all know what I'm talkin' 'bout.)

BUILDING YOUR INTIMACY "MUSCLES"

Love is never any better than the lover.

—Toni Morrison

Intimacy has been defined in romantic relationships as "the level of commitment and positive affective, cognitive, and physical closeness one experiences with a partner in a reciprocal (although not necessarily symmetrical) relationship."[5] This working definition of intimacy reveals that the cognitive, emotional, physical, and spiritual components of human nature are vital to building intimacy.[6] Therefore, to foster intimacy in our relationships, we are required to be intentional, communicative, and vulnerable. And that means consciously addressing all levels of intimacy. None can stand alone. All are required to build a healthy actualized relationship, as they all enhance the closeness between partners.

Relational exchanges build deep connections for sustained longevity in a healthy relationship. Relational discussions range from truth about the experiences of the day (not just saying, "I'm fine" or "It was good") to random reflections from childhood that impact your relationship to discussing who your current friends are. Since sex is an important element in intimacy, a lack of a cognitive presence strips sex of its power to create a truly intensified bonding experience. Relational sexual exchanges occur between two people who are interested in one another's pleasure. As a matter of fact, couples gain their greatest pleasure from cognitive, emotional, and spiritual intimacy well before reaching sexual pleasure. An unselfish partner will ensure the physical sexual experience is filled with pleasure at every level of physical intimate connection.

The key is vulnerability. Only by opening ourselves up can we connect on a deeper cognitive level, creating the ability to explore emotionality. Uninhibited openness is promoted by

---

5   Barry F. Moss and Andrew I. Schwebel, "Defining Intimacy in Romantic Relationships," *Family Relations* 42, no. 1 (January 1993): 31-37.

6   Moss and Schwebel, "Defining Intimacy," 31-37.

feelings of emotional safety and security. This is all wrapped in an understanding of your spirituality and core beliefs and values.

These components do not merely exist in human relationships, they have to be developed. I relate this development of intimate expression to the physicality of doing a 45-minute plank. While today it may be impossible for someone to hold a plank position for 45 minutes, building up to a 4- to 5-minute plank requires practice. Building up your intimacy muscle requires the same effort, fortitude, and practice.

CHAPTER 2

Expressions of Love and Intimacy

U nderstanding the different levels of intimacy as discussed in the previous chapter is one step toward finding better ways to connect with your partner. What is equally important is knowing that people express feelings of love, affection, and intimacy in different ways—they use different languages. We all express our feelings through verbal and non-verbal communication in different ways. If your partner is telling you they care about you in a language you don't understand, the message is completely lost.

When I work with clients around the love languages, I usually speak about the languages using a plant analogy. Imagine you have two plants. One is a cactus and the other a fern. They both have three basic needs: water, sunlight, and soil. However, the item that will either create growth or kill the plant is water. Too much for a cactus or too little for a fern and poof!, the plant is zapped of its power to be a beautiful, full, and fruitful creation. If you speak "cactus" to a fern, you'll kill it, and vice versa. In the same way, each partner in a couple needs a specific kind of love to develop into the greatest creation they can possibly be.

One of the models I think is helpful in teaching partners how to improve intimacy is called the **five love languages**, which was originally developed by Gary Chapman.[7] Now I know, many do not agree with Chapman's philosophies of life and find fault with the way in which he developed ideas around the five love languages. I will not argue those perspectives in this discussion. I will simply say that there are many couples I've worked with who have found his model to be useful to them in developing and expressing intimacy. According to Chapman, people will express their feelings of love and affection in one or more of the following five ways:

---

7   Gary Chapman, *The 5 Love Languages: How to Express Heartfelt Commitment to Your Mate* (Chicago: Northfield Publishing, 1992).

1. Words of affirmation

2. Quality time

3. Acts of service

4. Physical touch

5. Receiving gifts

Let's look at each of these in more depth. As you read the descriptions, think about which best apply to you and which language your partner might be using. We will share the assessment at the end so you can determine your specific language.

LOVE LANGUAGE #1: WORDS OF AFFIRMATION

Words of affirmation, as the label implies, are words that you use to show that you understand and appreciate your partner. They include:

- Compliments
- Words of appreciation or kindness
- Words of encouragement
- Compassion
- Kindness

Using words of affirmation does *not* mean saying something nice so you can get what you want from the other person. Complimenting someone else's behavior as an example of what your partner should do is not the way to use words of affirmation. You would not say, "See how well Mrs. X looks in that dress? That's what you should do," or "Mr. Y spends a lot of time with his children. Why don't you?"

Your partner would appreciate you telling them which dress does not make them look fat more than the attempt at sparing their feelings with "it's all right." A man might say, "Baby, that blue dress with the white vertical stripes makes you look so sexy to me. Let's wear blue tonight." See how he affirmed her? Or a woman might say, "You are an amazing example to our children of a great man. I love how gentle you are with them." See how she encouraged him?

If words of affirmation are your primary love language, hearing the words "I love you" are important—hearing the reasons behind that love means even more. Sometimes, you might even have to define love. Remember, our experiences help us make meaning. Unsolicited compliments mean the world to this partner. Insults can leave them shattered and are not easily forgotten. The Bible says, "Life and death are in the power of the tongue" (Proverbs 18:21). That means you get to determine the quality of the life you live in relationship.

If you want to improve intimacy with a partner whose primary love language is words of affirmation, know that your words can instill courage and confidence. That encouragement must be focused on what your partner wants, not on manipulating them to do what you desire.

Here are some simple ways to include words of affirmation in your day-to-day life:

- Remember that words are important
- Set a goal to compliment your partner daily
- Watch your tone of voice

- Make requests, not demands
- Compliment your partner in the presence of others, not just in private

See below for some quick examples of how to use these tips. There is also an affirmations worksheet in Appendix A (Tools) if this is an area you would like to explore further.

EVERYDAY EXAMPLES OF AFFIRMATION

- Thank your partner for cooking a tasty meal.
- Congratulate them for hitting a weight loss milestone or achieving a workout goal.
- Leave an encouraging note when they have a big presentation at work.
- Remind them of how capable they are when they doubt themselves.
- Compliment their outfit, hair, or something else about their appearance.
- Hide a card with a loving message in their suitcase when they're going on a trip.
- Send them a text just to say you were thinking of them.

For more examples of words that express affirmation, see Appendix A (Tools).

LOVE LANGUAGE #2: QUALITY TIME

I'm betting you know what quality time means without me having to define it. You know I am going to anyway. As a matter of fact, you will need to ask your partner what this means to them. In essence, it is spending time with each other, without being distracted by external forces. To people who use this language, nothing says, "I love you," like giving or receiving full, undivided attention when they are with another person and then experiencing these deeply emotional exchanges that create everlasting connections. For them, distractions, postponed dates, judging emotional exchanges, dismissing perspectives, or the failure to listen during quality time can be especially hurtful.

A central aspect of quality time is togetherness. I do not mean proximity. Togetherness has to do with focused attention and intentionality. Your mind and body turn toward your partner; you listen and respond with the purpose of remembering. A husband who is watching sports on television while he talks to his wife is not giving her quality time, because she does not have his full attention. The same could be said for a wife who is more focused on preparing a meal or getting dressed than she is listening to her husband.

To qualify as quality time, both parties are really present when they are together—the TV is off, fork and knife are down if at a meal, all chores and tasks are on standby, no electronic devices are present to provide distractions. You are both doing an activity you enjoy (or one enjoys and the other is willing to do) to be together—the emphasis is not so much on *what* you are doing but on *why*.

Quality time can also include quality conversation, which means a sympathetic dialogue where two people are sharing their experiences, their thoughts, their feelings, and their desires in a friendly, uninterrupted context. Quality conversation is crucial to this partner's emotional sense of being loved. To have a quality conversation with someone to whom quality time is important:

- Sit down and be still (mentally and emotionally) when you are talking with your partner.

- Ask non-judgmental questions.

- Listen to both what they are saying and how they are saying it. The feelings expressed through words and actions are an important component of communication.

- Refuse to interrupt.

- Be willing to share your own feelings, wishes, and dreams.

- When your spouse asks to talk to you about something, put your smart phone or iPad down and make eye contact with them while they speak.

EVERYDAY EXAMPLES OF QUALITY TIME

- Make date night a weekly event. Even if you can't afford a babysitter, plan a night at home that is yours alone.

- Have coffee together before work.

- After work, set aside 10 minutes to catch up—no phones allowed.

- Always maintain eye contact when you're having a conversation.

- Go to bed at the same time, if possible.

- Plan a staycation.

- Go to bed at the same time, even if at times you have to get up after they've fallen asleep. It's meaningful for your partner to know that you are spending that time with them right before you sleep together.

- Go for walks together after dinner. Even if the kids join you, the time spent will mean a lot.

LOVE LANGUAGE #3: ACTS OF SERVICE

Can vacuuming the floors really be an expression of love? Absolutely! Anything you do to ease the burden of responsibilities weighing on your partner will speak volumes if you are using the language of acts of service.

Put simply, acts of service is love expressed by actions. People who speak this love language primarily seek to be pleased by their partner serving them; for the partner to express their love for them by doing things for them. And they appreciate when they are acknowledged for being the giver of such acts as well. They pay attention to how much thought, time, energy, and effort goes into an action that benefits either them (as giver) or their partner (as receiver).

The person who is nourished by acts of service can be devastated, feel forgotten, crushed, and unloved if their partner exudes laziness, continually puts the brakes on commitments, and creates more work for them. It is as though their feelings don't matter.

Whether the giver or receiver of acts of service, actions must be done with a positive spirit to be a true expression of love. I'm not saying become a slave to your partner and do these things out of guilt or resentment; no person should ever be a doormat. Just do things that will benefit your partner because you love them. It will benefit you when your partner expresses appreciation for your kindness. And hey, according to research conducted by Dr. John Gottman at the University of Washington, women are more likely to get in the mood when men help out with the housework! So if you really want some HBNS (Hot Butt Naked Sex) you might try working out through housework and see if you get a rise.

If your partner uses acts of service as their main language:

- The words he or she most want to hear are: "Let me do that for you."

- Do anything that requires thought, planning, time, effort, and energy (see below for some suggestions).

- Tell your spouse you're going to take over one of their dreaded chores.

- Be quick to do whatever your spouse asks you to do for them.

- Ask your spouse, "What is the most meaningful thing I do for you?" and then, as much as you're able to, always faithfully do it.

- Find something unexpected you can do that will make them smile.

EVERYDAY EXAMPLES OF ACTS OF SERVICE

- Cook a meal or pack a lunch.
- Set the table.
- Wash the dishes.
- Sort the bills.
- Walk the dog.
- Get their car washed.
- Pick up their dry cleaning.
- Fill up their gas tank.
- Do the laundry.

continued

- Keep a short list of repairs needed around the house and fix them as time allows.
- If they need to bring a present to a party or event, help by picking it out or purchasing it for them.

LOVE LANGUAGE #4: PHYSICAL TOUCH

We all have a need to have physical touch in our lives, from the time we are infants to our last breath. Lack of physical contact is why so many people were challenged mentally and emotionally during the pandemic. The isolation was palpable. It opened our society to bouts of anxiety, mild depression, and increased anger.

The love language of physical touch can be uncomfortable for those who grew up in families who did not hug or display affection outwardly. So if your partner grows through physical touch and you are repulsed by touch, therapy is important.

People who express love in this way have a greater need than others for physical touch. And this isn't all about sex, though sex is an important aspect of touch. It may include hugs, holding hands, a brief touch of one's shoulder, thoughtful touches on the arm, a hand on the knee, or a brief kiss before leaving home. To people for whom physical touch is the primary language of love, physical presence and accessibility are crucial.

If you partner's primary love language is physical touch:

- Touch him or her even when you're not having sex: hold hands, kiss, hug. All of these are lifelines. With them your partner feels secure in your love.

- However, don't forget the sex!
- Sit close to your partner as you watch TV, rub their feet—this requires no additional time and the bare minimum of effort, but communicates your love loudly.

If touching is NOT your primary love language, or you didn't grow up in a "touching" family, you may struggle to meet the needs of a partner who uses this language. Keep in mind that "love touches" don't take much time, but they do require a little thought. You don't want to touch your mate in ways that trigger unpleasant thoughts or that are unwanted at times.

EVERYDAY EXAMPLES OF PHYSICAL TOUCH

- Hold your spouse's hand whenever you're out walking together, whether in the mall, at the beach, or around the block.
- Kiss your spouse often. Make it a point to greet them at the door with a hug and a kiss. Do the same when they're leaving for the day.
- Hold or hug your partner without saying a word; just because.
- Cuddle together in bed.
- Give your partner regular neck, back, foot, or full-body massages. Buy various lotions and oils to make this even more of a treat.
- When driving, rubbing a knee or hand gently builds connection.

LOVE LANGUAGE #5: RECEIVING GIFTS

Almost everything ever written on the subject of love indicates that at the heart of love is the spirit of giving. All five love languages challenge us to give to our spouse, but for some receiving gifts, visible symbols of love, speaks the loudest. A gift is something you can hold in your hand and say, "Look, he was thinking of me," or "She remembered me." A gift is a symbol of that thought. Gifts come in all sizes, colors, and shapes. Some are expensive and others are *free*. To the individual whose primary love language is receiving gifts, the cost will matter based on the occasion, socio-economic status, and experience—this is what satisfies the need. You must know your partner in every language, but with gifts in particular. Why? Because if your language is words of affirmation and you purchase a gift that is not "appropriate," both you and your partner's languages may be missed. They will not praise your efforts or be fulfilled by the gift you offered.

Don't mistake this love language for materialism; the receiver of gifts thrives on the love, thoughtfulness, and effort behind the gift. If you speak this language, the perfect gift or gesture shows that you are seen (known and understood), you are cared for, and you are prized above whatever was sacrificed to bring the gift to you. A missed birthday, anniversary, or a hasty, thoughtless gift would be disastrous—so would the absence of everyday gestures.

If your partner's primary love language is receiving gifts:

- Give them small gifts often. These do NOT have to be big or expensive purchases. It could be as simple as flowers, a card, floor mats for the car, a subscription to a magazine or a regular car wash, dinner, or a baseball. To your partner, the active of giving has little to do with monetary value and everything to do with love! If you have time, wrap the item or present it in a special way.

- Remember that gifts do not have to be physical items that people can hold in their hands—holding hands can be a gift in itself. Often the gift of your *presence* will be the best *present* your partner can receive, especially during times of distress or crisis and joy and excitement.

EVERYDAY EXAMPLES OF RECEIVING GIFTS

- Buy your partner concert tickets when their favorite band or performer is in town.
- Peruse their Pinterest page and purchase an item they've pinned.
- Create an email where they can send gift ideas with links to make it easy to order or schedule.
- After a trip, bring home a souvenir or trinket that made you think of them.
- Order their favorite childhood candy or snack—bonus points if it's a regional treat or something that has since been discontinued.
- Keep a note in your phone of specific things they mention wanting or needing so you have a list of gift ideas for birthdays, anniversaries, holidays, or just because.

SPEAKING EACH OTHER'S LOVE LANGUAGES

When Black couples do not understand that there can be other forms of expression apart from their favorite ones, achieving intimacy will continue to be a problem in their relationship. That's why it's important to recognize that everyone has a primary love language—their natural or preferred way of expressing affection.

Many of us will have a secondary language, behaviors or words that we *recognize* as expressions of love even if we don't use that language very often.

Raymond, whose primary love language is physical touch, and Rachel, whose primary language is acts of service, had intense conversations about the meaning of their primary love languages for their relationship. Then began intentionally practicing specific acts that increased their connection across cognitive, emotional, and spiritual intimacy. Eventually, Raymond received random acts of sexual touch and pleasure that even Rachel enjoyed. Raymond found himself eager to complete acts of service for Rachel because he found joy in seeing her glow with affection for not only him but also for their children.

As time went on they tapped into their secondary language, which happened to be the same, quality time. Quality time allowed them to enhance their intimacy. When challenges presented themselves, they were better able to communicate, re-negotiate expectations, set new boundaries, and find ways to compromise. The ebbs and flows in their relationship came with the territory. Their ability to work through them came with the new ways they had learned by being intimate with each other.

As with Raymond and Rachel, it's common for a couple to have different primary love languages. Luckily it is not necessary to have the exact same love language in order to find compatibility. Differing love languages mean that in order to increase intimacy, you will have to stretch yourself so you speak the language that your partner will understand (and vice versa). Again, this is loosely based on scientific research. There are certainly many ways to connect with your partner. You can discover those with intentionality and energy and sometimes therapy.

There is a love languages worksheet in Appendix A (Tools) to help you identify which language(s) you and your partner prefer. But to get you started, review the descriptions above. Which sounded most like you? What do you ask your partner to do to express their love—hold hands? Do a household chore? Simply sit with you and talk? Based on what you want to see in your relationship, what do you think is your primary or preferred love language?

Now think about your partner. Which descriptions sound most like them? What things do they appreciate? What do they ask for? What annoys them? These give you clues, but you don't have to guess! Communicate, ask questions about what your partner likes and doesn't like, be assertive in expressing your own needs.

Identifying your partner's primary language is not always easy. Honestly, we have a tendency to be self-centered beings. Oftentimes, it's easier to identify, discuss, and share your own love language than to fully understand what language your partner is manifesting. The challenge is especially true when things have been bad in the relationship for some time or when they are using your love language to hurt you rather than support you. If you have a hard time identifying what your spouse does that makes you feel loved, ask yourself the opposite question: what do they *fail* to do that hurts you deeply?

Once you have identified your own and your partner's love languages, speak up and ask for what you need. Offer your partner the words and actions *they* will understand as expressions of affection. If it's not clear what languages you each use, take the assessment to find what works for you. Recognize that over time—particularly as you age—love languages can change.

CHAPTER 3

The Barriers to Intimacy in Black Couples

What everyone wants more than anything else is to be loved.

—Ella Fitzgerald

T here are many factors that impact how relationships and intimacy are viewed in the Black culture, many of them creating barriers to intimacy in Black couples. Unfortunately, over the decades, Black sexuality has largely been framed in terms of negative narratives, encouraged by a biased and racist perspective that undervalues the Black experience. I believe there is misrepresentation of Black love/sexuality as Black people's inability or unwillingness to build intimate and committed relationships.

In this chapter, I want to explore some of the main factors in history and society that make it hard for many Black couples to develop the intimacy they seek.

THE LASTING IMPACT OF SLAVERY

Much of what is not studied and therefore is unacknowledged in Black relationship intimacy is related to the racist history of the United States: slavery, Jim Crow (old and new), the school-to-prison pipeline, systemic racism, and various aspects of the Civil Rights era. These historical factors have had a lasting legacy on the Black family's ability to build sustainable relationships.

Research[8] has demonstrated that much of the animosity between Black males and females is connected to slavery. More directly, to the capitalism of slavery. Slave masters needed more hands to work on their farms, so they forced Black male slaves to impregnate Black female slaves for procreation to increase their financial gain. The children and parents were ultimately separated when one or the other was sold to another plantation. Rarely did the father know much about the child and if he tried to protect either the child or woman, he was punished severely. This practice of forcibly separating parents and children allowed the slave owners a means of control over the slaves. Rarely was a family unit allowed to stay intact. Those that were allowed to marry could have their union destroyed with the slightest infraction. If slaves developed intimate relationships with each other, they were kept secret. Thus, it became difficult for slaves to maintain intimate relationships. And there was little to no representation of healthy intimate relationships.

Additionally, White slave owners often raped Black female slaves. To be especially cruel, they would make Black male slaves

---

8   S.E. Anderson and Rosemari Mealy, "Who Originated the Crises? A Historical Perspective," *The Black Scholar* 10, no. 8/9 (May/June 1979): 40-67.

who were possibly protectors watch. The female and male slaves were infuriated and felt helpless and hopeless. These rapes also worked to destroy Black intimate relationships. They pitted male and female slaves against one another, even as both recognized there was little either could do about their circumstances. Many times, for survival, they had no choice but to betray their hearts and turn against each other.

It has been said that during slavery, the psychological development of Black male survival required them to despise the Black woman.[9] The Black man likely hated his inability to protect her but projected the anger it produced toward the Black woman, easing its impact on the need to serve the White man.

As time progressed, Black males often took their frustrations out on Black women who were already being violated. Females learned not to trust Black men. Once again, in multiple situations, White slave masters, and eventually racist institutions, would sever the relationships, effectively demolishing the ability to build intimacy between Black men and women—even from infancy.[10]

Given this lasting legacy of slavery and racism, it's no wonder that Black women have often been seen as angry, bullies, strong, weak, unintelligent, inferior, vulnerable, and prone to hysteria or that Black men have been seen as angry, cold-hearted, lacking emotional vulnerability, poor providers, oversexed, strong,

9   Jennifer Hallam, "Slavery and the Making of America," PBS, 2004, Educational Broadcasting Corporation, accessed August 16, 2022, https://www.thirteen.org/wnet/slavery/experience/family/p_history.html.

10   Robert Staples, "Masculinity and Race: The Dual Dilemma of Black Men," *Journal of Social Issues* 34, no. 1 (Winter 1978): 169-181.

deadbeats, and philanderers. Yep, all that wrapped in one! Imagine the conflict we create within ourselves if we believe such labels to be true. With all of this history and the systematic denigration of Black existence, how can true knowledge of intimacy be gained, implemented, and practiced?

FINANCIAL INSTABILITY AND THE ONGOING IMPACT OF RACISM

Financial stability is often treated as the cornerstone of the Black family. The Bible says that "money answers all things" (Ecclesiastes 10:19). It is a goal that is challenging for many Black individuals and families because of the previous and current racism in this country.

In fact, the social and economic status of a Black couple or family is directly connected to their ability to navigate the institutional racism that exists throughout the world, but particularly in America. Even 160 years after Emancipation, many Black men are still stripped of their ability to receive quality education, healthcare, to participate in politics and policy-making, and few have seats at the tables of boardrooms or lead companies in corporate America. No wonder they feel emasculated, undermined in their ability to provide for themselves and their families.

Researchers confirm the idea that bad economic challenges in the home contribute to the Black male's perception of Black females. Researchers say the stress from work, competition with a partner, parenting, and conflicts—both familial and societal—create anger, disappointment, feelings of rejection, and a need for release in Black men that is demonstrated in maladaptive behaviors.

Further, there are a plethora of firsthand documented experiences where the government literally told Black families that in order to receive assistance (financial, medical, or otherwise), they would need to remove the Black father from the home. Thus, the government was complicit in creating the single-parent household and then stigmatized the mothers for having children out of wedlock or fathers for being deadbeat dads.

The impact of these economic and social factors on intimacy is clear: Black men may not decide to have close intimate relationships because they believe they cannot provide at the societal levels required by the Black woman. They may self-soothe their depression with multiple sexual relationships, in an effort not to demonstrate vulnerability. These behaviors strip Black women of any alternative but to fill the gaps left in Black families. In partnerships, both male and female become aggravated, angry, or they feel forgotten, mistrusting and potentially disliking the other. Over time, feeding the narrative of dysfunctional Black intimate relationships further alienates Black men from Black women and ultimately from a powerful union.

When people are precluded from producing wealth in this society, they are also removed from being able to answer the call for true intimacy. I know this connection may be a stretch for some, but imagine what the Black couple relationship would look like with the ease of financial *stability* available without the sting of racism.

MODERN CULTURAL CONDITIONING

As if the impact of historical conditions including slavery and
bad economic policy weren't enough, there are ongoing forces
in American culture that continue to work against Black intimacy. The cultural conditioning of the collective attitudes,
beliefs, and cultural messages in our society—which have been
largely based on the White culture's biases—have been, and still
are, accepted even within the Black community. These pressures
from a collective whole have impacted the ways in which Black
people experience and project intimacy in their relationships.

In one study, for example, eighty percent of the college students who participated reported that the media influences on
their relationships were more impactful than parental influence.[11]
That is not a shocker, right? As young adults experience many
transitions—graduating from high school, completing college,
changing jobs, and moving to new apartments or houses—the
media has a strong influence on how they explore, construct, and
express their identity.[12]

Much of the research explores how anti-Black narratives, stereotypes, and messages transmitted through media also have a profound
impact on how Black individuals perceive and interact with each

---

11 Pamela B. Trotter, "The Influence of Parental Romantic Relationships on College
    Students' Attitudes about Romantic Relationships," *College Student Journal*, 44, no.
    1 (2010): 71-83.

12 Sarah M. Coyne, Laura M. Padilla-Walker, and Emily Howard, "Emerging in a
    Digital World: A Decade Review of Media Use, Effects, and Gratifications in
    Emerging Adulthood," *Emerging Adulthood* 1, no. 2 (June 2013): 125-137, https://
    doi:10.1177/2167696813479782.

other.[13] TV programs like *The Cosby Show* and *Black-ish* attempt to combat the negative narrative, but these positive models are few and far between. Kelly and Floyd's study determined that negative narratives of Black couples in media and culture decreased relationship intimacy by forty-three percent. This study actually found that couples perceived their partner to be less dependable, less trustworthy, and that it decreased their satisfaction with their partner overall based on their cultural conditioning through media.

All media and other entertainment industries should be interested in telling positive narratives of Black identity and culture. Despite initiatives to display Black relationships in a positive light with shows like the ones mentioned above, research has demonstrated that even the hip-hop culture has watered down the quality and stability of Black relationships through negative images and stereotypes.[14] Although early hip-hop culture had a positive influence on Black identity and sexuality, negative stereotypes crept in during the 1990s and that began to shift the paradigm.[15] Hip-hop encourages a type of emotional closeness and intimacy between men that is often at

13 Shalonda Kelly and Frank J. Floyd, "The Effects of Negative Racial Stereotypes and Afro-centricity on Black Couple Relationships," *Journal of Family Psychology* 15, no. 1 (March 2001): 110-23, https://doi:10.1037/0893-3200.15.1.110.

14 David Stamps, "The Social Construction of the African American Family on Broadcast Television: A Comparative Analysis of *The Cosby Show* and *Blackish*," *Howard Journal of Communications* 28, no. 4 (June 2017): 405-420, https://doi:10.1 080/10646175.2017.1315688.

15 Dionne Patricia Stephens, "The Influence of Mainstream Hip Hop's Female Sexual Scripts on African American Women's Dating Relationship Experiences," in *The Psychology of Love*, ed. M. Paludi (Santa Barbara: Praeger Publishing, 2012), 69-83.

the expense of their relationships with women. Music further perpetuates barriers between the two genders through the lens of sexual objectification and ruthless male stereotypes of abusive behaviors. Eventually, even women began to use music to combat the sexual onslaught. There are myriad songs from the 1970s to the present day that attempt to give women their sexual power back.

Hip-hop was not expected to give a fresh narrative of Black intimacy, identity, or sexuality. The Black family was. Several movies have fed us with pitiful and dysfunctional representations of Black intimacy, identity, and sexuality. Young Black adults watch these movies and they are led to believe that Black marriages and positive romantic relationships simply do not exist within Black culture. Instead, young adults are overwhelmed with images of a bullied man/woman, the nagging wife, an indifferent husband, the promiscuous partner, and the teary/anxious/abused partner. We also see the representation of Black parents as poor parental role models: their children are rowdy and badly raised, the parents are concerned with peddling drugs, are doing time in prison, or are hawking sex and engaging in prostitution. The few times we see powerful Black families in action is mostly short-lived. Rarely is there a Hallmark-like movie that depicts a Black couple that establishes a solid romantic relationship by working through the struggle of intimacy or socioeconomic distress.

Considering the context of hip-hop culture and media presentation, Black couple intimacy is depicted as hyper-sexualized—Black men and women are portrayed as animalistic in their sexual desires and as having little to no control over their sexual urges. Often, because the community has no input in creating the narratives, these representations do not give Black couples the opportunity or the needed platform to define a positive Black identity or positive romantic relationships.

CULTURAL FEAR OF VULNERABILITY

Love is a battle; love is a war; love is a growing up.

—James Baldwin

The history, social conditioning, media, and societal norms of Black families and their intimacy has created a culture where vulnerability is unacceptable. Yet to achieve true intimacy, you must open yourself to the full expression of emotion. Vulnerability is a form of self-acceptance. To become vulnerable means you are willing to fully express your personality, insecurities, and flaws. We have to set aside the notion of the strong woman with no time to be sitting around crying about her troubles. We have to dismantle the idea that a man in touch with his deepest hopes, fears, and desires is somehow a punk for expressing them. As a culture, we must acknowledge that vulnerability is required to establish an intimate relationship.

Unfortunately, being vulnerable can be kryptonite in the Black community. Culturally, both Black men and Black women struggle with the exposure of raw emotion. Generally speaking, men struggle with greater intensity than women and for different reasons. As a matter of fact, I'm convinced the commercial for Dry Idea deodorant was marketed to the Black community. You know the saying "Never let them see you sweat." Now ask

yourself, what part of your intimate relationship do you sweat
about? What do you do to cover that up?

I've heard these beliefs over and over again in my practice.
For example, Raymond was a client from Washington, DC. He
grew up in the southeast section of the city, which had a reputa-
tion for being a particularly dangerous neighborhood. Raymond
told me that for as long as he could remember Black boys were
taught from childhood to be strong: "don't be a punk," "man up."
When children in these communities were hurt emotionally and
sometimes physically, they were asked . . . and we've all heard it
before, "You want me to give you something to cry about?" or
told, "Get somewhere and sit down," "Children should be seen
and not heard," or "Get over it." Raymond made it clear that he
knew that showing any type of emotion other than anger was a
sign of weakness and it could get you killed.

I have found that this same concept is taught universally
throughout the Black community. Through my experience as a
relationship expert, I have discovered that not many of the Black
men I have counseled were ever encouraged to express emotions beyond the willingness to fight. Consequently, they find it
challenging to access feelings of love, affection, adoration, loneliness, acceptance, rejection, humility, contentment, depression,
anxiety, brokenness, vibrancy, animation, satisfaction, or being
forgotten—which are just a few of the emotions available to us
as human beings, as I talked about in chapter 1. There is no way
to effectively communicate without emotion. Without understanding our feelings, acknowledging that we feel them, and
embracing them, we become mute. There is no way to effectively
communicate without emotion.

The society we live in also requires that we not be emotional. We can't demonstrate passion or we become the "mad Black woman" or the "angry Black man."[16] White women can be fragile and even cry at work, while Black women have to faint to receive the same level of empathy.

There are other cultural issues within the Black community that are stifling the Black couple's ability to express their desires for sexual connection. For example, fewer Black women perform oral sex than women in any other culture. Similarly, many couples I've worked with can attest that it was not acceptable to be too unique when discussing sexual escapades with their support group, partner, or community. Many Black men speak of being taught it was their role to "bring the hammer," "get in them guts," or "beat the pussy" in the bedroom. None of the aforementioned perspectives present a sex-positive approach to intimacy. If they brought flowers and courted a young woman for a few months before having sex, they were called "soft" or "whupped."

Sound familiar? Ask yourself, how often were you rewarded for telling the truth about your feelings or expressing a point of view on intimacy or sex that didn't align with cultural or religious expectations. Did you understand emotions beyond anger, sadness, or happiness? Were the relationships around you abusive in any way (physically, emotionally, psychologically, verbally)?

Now, ask yourself, are you living in the relationship you want or the relationship of your mother and father, grandparents,

---

16 Janice P. Gump, PhD, "Reality Matters: The Shadow of Trauma on African American Subjectivity," *Psychoanalytic Psychology* 27, no. 1 (2010): 42-54, https://doi:10.1037/a0018639.

pastor, barber, your boys, or your girlfriends? Is that a place you want to be?

Vulnerability is not for the faint-hearted because none of us can know how expressions of our true selves will be received. An example of this level of vulnerability existed with my client who revealed to his wife that he was raped by a male family friend repeatedly between ages seven and twelve. She expressed genuine sadness that her husband had been violated. Feeling safe, he opened up further and explained that sometimes he is uncomfortable with some of their sexual activities (anal play, oral sex, and porn) because they remind him of that time in his life. His wife was taken aback. She immediately scowled and began to berate him about possibly being gay. He denied any connection to being homosexual and shut down. The honesty, generosity, and awareness that brought about a depth of vulnerability, that transformed intimacy, was broken. (I'll talk more about vulnerability and creating safe environments for open, honest communication in later chapters.)

ACKNOWLEDGING AND TEARING DOWN THE BARRIERS

Intimacy among Black couples is an under-researched field, and the assumptions our culture utilizes to fanaticize Black intimacy are grossly erroneous and should be further challenged with additional, extensive research, surveys, and studies.

In the meantime, it's clear that there are a number of factors at play that are erecting barriers to intimacy in Black couples: a lack of communication, mistrust, a lack of vulnerability, and dysfunctional relational development, just to name a few. The origin of these barriers to intimacy can be found in gender differences, socioeconomic challenges, institutional racism, and more than anything, generational history. These are by no means the only barriers that exist, but to dismantle them it is imperative that we recognize, openly acknowledge, and understand them.

I acknowledge that especially in the Black community, understanding and acknowledging our fears and vulnerability would be easier if there were no historical roadblocks that had funneled our expectations into narrow avenues. But the more knowledge we have about the historical and cultural forces working against Black intimacy, the better equipped we will be to learn how to turn our individual narratives toward building healthy intimate relationships with our partners.

CHAPTER 4

The Narratives that Shape Our Behavior

Love in such a way that the person you love feels free.

—Thich Nhat Hanh

Adrian is a heterosexual Black male. He has been emotionally and sexually involved with a good number of women. Sexually active since age fourteen, Adrian is now thirty-six years old, and within the past six years, he has been romantically involved with four women and has been sexually involved with fifteen. Adrian is sexually expressive, and any woman who doesn't understand his sexual language will be unable to fill his love tank. He wanted desperately to be married and have a family.

Then Adrian met Mia, a 37-year-old heterosexual Black female who believes in building emotional support and

companionship in an intimate relationship. She met Adrian at
a book launch and they agreed to go out for coffee. During one
of the many dates that followed in quick succession, Mia mentioned that she prefers baking pastries with her boyfriend on
Friday nights to clubbing. She also mentioned that she prefers
pillow talk and cuddling to sex.

The idea of staying home on a Friday night and cuddling are outside
Adrian's "relationship script"—the inner narratives we all have that
shape how we behave and what we expect to happen in our romantic
relationships. Relationship scripts reflect our established norms, patterns, choices, desires, fears, and thoughts for a relationship. They are
our models of how relationships work: how previous ones worked and
how the current and subsequent ones *will* work. That is why when we
begin a new relationship, we often expect a particular pattern to unfold.
Hence, when X happens, we expect that Y will follow.

Adrian acknowledged that he enjoyed the calmness of Mia's
presence, and he knew that she could give him peace of mind.
But his relationship script was built around his sexual appetite;
it did not incorporate the kind of cognitive and emotional intimacy that Mia demonstrated. He was uncomfortable with her
desire for deep discussions and did not enjoy talking about his
family or upbringing.

Mia eventually realized she and Adrian had no connection
beyond sexual attraction. She told this to Adrian, and he became
defensive. Instinctively, Adrian began to give Mia excuses about

why they couldn't spend time with each other, and with time Mia understood that he was avoiding her.

In short, Adrian had a relationship script that prevented him from doing the emotional work needed to achieve his goal. Adrian did not *have* to be doomed by the pattern he created. He could have learned how to make better choices when it came to building intimacy with his partner. That would have taken time and effort, and Mia would have been willing to commit to the intentional effort of re-scripting. But Adrian became a victim of his own narrative, and his behavior sabotaged his chance at intimacy with Mia.

In principle, relationship scripts are wonderful things to have. We perform most of our emotional work with them. With positive scripts, we can write and practice what is desired in the most excellent, healthy relationship we desire. Just as a movie producer will have that perfect story they want to turn into a movie and they know the right cast to work with to bring the story alive. But if they do not script the story well, even the most efficient cast might mess the plot up. This is the same with emotional work.

Because of the racial history, cultural conditioning, and generational influences described in the previous chapter, the relationship scripts that shape the behavior of Black couples can be destructive to intimacy rather than encouraging. Short clips on Instagram and Facebook that explain what a man or woman will do if they love or want to be with you do not take into account the relationship scripts of each individual. They provide blanket ideas that are popular and ignore the fact that work is required to understand how each partner's individuality relates to the desire to become a couple. For example, there are popular memes that tell us "A man does not love you if he is not calling you in the morning, mid-morning, afternoon, mid-afternoon, evening, and just before midnight, basically every four hours." This may not be best for your relationship.

As I mentioned in the previous chapter, stories that feature positive intimate relationships in Black communities, and which could create a more positive relationship script, are few and far between in the media and society. Growing research on romantic relationships and the impact of relationship scripts on Black-couple intimacy has highlighted a widening difference between how Black men and women internalize relationship scripts and how these scripts affect their desire to attain cognitive, emotional, spiritual, and sexual satisfaction in their relationships. Romantic attachments work differently for both genders. The research also revealed how such negative narrative scripts inform and sabotage their desires for true intimacy.[17]

In this chapter, I want to examine common relationship scripts I hear about from both men and women in the Black community, showing how they impede true intimacy, and discussing how we can learn to reframe negative scripts to build more positive models for intimacy for Black couples.

---

17 Lisa Bowleg, Kenya J. Lucas, and Jeanne M. Tschann, "'The Ball Was Always in His Court': An Exploratory Analysis of Relationship Scripts, Sexual Scripts, and Condom Use among African American Women," *Psychology of Women Quarterly* 28, no. 1 (March 2004): 70-82, https://doi:10.1111/j.1471-6402.2004.00124.x.

SOCIAL LEARNING: WHAT WE OBSERVE, WE REPEAT

One way to examine what shapes our understanding of intimacy is through the lens of social learning theory: we learn by observing others. Those "others" are all the people in our social circle: parents and grandparents, siblings, friends, our larger community. We identify the core beliefs of the people around us through discussion and behavior. Then we decide what we desire to imitate or disavow. As a result, we either reinforce or change our behaviors as we discover and create our own belief systems (spiritual), worldview (cognitive), and emotional connection to those beliefs and views. Each of us then takes these beliefs, emotions, and worldviews into a relationship, influencing how we feel about and respond to our partner's words and actions.

Studies have revealed that young adults are strongly influenced by the relationship between their parents or the relationships in close proximity to them during childhood.[18] It is a given fact that these parents were also influenced by the relationships between their parents and on back through the generations. As a result, the ways in which family members establish and communicate their emotional process, attitudes, values, and beliefs are handed down over the decades.[19]

This generational influence is not always positive: we all know families that sweep everything under the carpet. Those of us who grew up in such households knew better than to take

---

18   Jasmine A. Abrams, PhD; Morgan L. Maxwell, PhD; and Faye Z. Belgrave, PhD, "Circumstances Beyond Their Control: Black Women's Perceptions of Black Manhood," *Sex Roles* 79, no. 3-4 (2018): 151-162, https://doi:10.1007/s11199-017-0870-8.

19   Michael E. Kerr, MD; and Murray Bowen, MD, *Family Evaluation* (New York: W.W. Norton & Company, 1988).

our business in the streets. You know what I'm talking about, right? If we saw our uncle kiss another woman (other than the aunt we grew up thinking he was married to) and told our mothers, we would be reprimanded for telling someone else's business. (Later in life we find out that woman he was kissing was his legal wife and the woman we thought was our aunt wasn't. Oooh, am I preaching to the choir?) This pattern of keeping family secrets discourages intimacy.

This is normal in many intimate Black relationships. Researchers who explored family messages revealed that young adult Black women received the bulk of their sexual socialization from both male and female family members, whereas Black men received theirs from the male family members only. This socialization and demonstration of the cultural norms accepted within and outside the family can't help but shape young Black adult views on sex and relationships.

Dysfunctional family systems are a barrier to Black-couple intimacy. The family is the first place of socialization for the child and is a hub of intimacy, in whatever way it shows up. In many families, there is a deeply enriching connection between marriages and generations that show genuine affection and adoration. The family works diligently to represent longevity in relationships. Then there are families that cannot see their way through the fog, the fog of damage, trauma, and grief and the longing for what a healthy relationship looks like. Ultimately, the community's lack of intimacy invariably rubs off on generations of children who have no ability to be vulnerable. Thus, to tackle the barrier of intimacy in Black-couple relationships, Black males and females need to begin seeing healthy intimate relationships. If we have no healthy relationships to imitate, then we must *learn* the skills to model for generations to come. It is true that some Black couples may have been socialized to be distrustful of each other in relationships due to family, societal, and cultural messages.[20] And to reprogram this teaching, Black couples should be intentional in their commitment to build intimacy. The greatest generational wealth we can leave is mental and emotional wellness.

GENDER EXPECTATIONS

Another huge factor that shapes what we expect from intimate relationships has to do with how we think about the roles of men and women.

Understanding gender differences may seem like a no-brainer. We recognize that men and women are not only physically different but also mentally and emotionally different. Researching history, we see that for centuries we were taught that the woman is the weaker sex. Even in most religious settings, scriptures are interpreted in that way. Laws that have governed many societies throughout history favor men at the expense of women. Shoot, our immediate reality has men attempting to regulate women's reproductive choices. Considering the specific historical conditions of Black men and women, it's not surprising that each has very different expectations in terms of how relationships could,

---

20 Christiana I. Ijeoma and Ijeoma Opara, "Socioemotional Factor: A Missing Gap in Theorizing and Studying Black Heterosexual Coupling Processes and Relationships," *Journal of Black Sexuality and Relationships* 3, no. 2 (2016): 25-51, https://doi: 10.1353/bsr.2016.0027.

should, or ought to work. The questions become, who said and is that what is right for you and your relationship?

The challenges of gender roles between Black couples are made greater because of the conflicting messages that each person receives through social learning. Every day Black women and men hear contradictory messages, directly and indirectly, from older Black adults as a warning, advice, or as preparatory counsel for the travails Black males and females are going to face being in a relationship with each other.

The conflicting messages sent to Black women are:

- To be self-reliant because their world is a difficult place where it will be almost impossible to find a Black man who will have the willingness and capability to take care of them. This message would have been an eye-opener if the instructors had instructed Black women to think outside the confines of romantic relationships, if they had told them that they needed to be independent to take care of themselves and to build their self-confidence by being resourceful. The message should have emphasized the need to be productive as an adult and not as someone who needed to be taken care of.

- The second message to Black females contradicts the first. This message tells Black females to be conscious of their attitude so that they can find and keep a Black man. It reaffirms the age-old belief that the ultimate achievement of a heterosexual woman is the presence of a man in their lives to complete them. This would have been a resourceful message if males were taught the same thing. That way, both parties would move around with the consciousness that they complement each other in a romantic relationship.

Black men hear the following conflicting messages:

- They are constantly urged to "become a man." In this sense, becoming a man means that a Black man must be domineering, aggressive, decisive, responsible, and (in some cases) violent in certain encounters with people to prove their manliness. The Black male was taught that power and ego define a man. Whereas this teaching is right, the second aspect of it contradicts the message of the first and drastically shatters the confidence of the Black male. Hence, he becomes an embodiment of entitlement and bruised ego.

- On the other hand, Black males are told they shouldn't be too aggressive and dominant, lest the system cut them down. When the Black male is moving around with the conflicting identity created by these messages, the Black female in their life suffers because of it.

With all these conflicting messages, it's no wonder that Black men and women often have confusing scripts in their head about how relationships should work.

The Relationship Scripts of Black Women

Long before they become romantically or sexually involved with a partner, Black women receive messages from family members that warn them about how men's relationship behaviors focus on sex, a lack of commitment, and emotional abandonment. In general, growing up Black girls encounter messages—from Disney movies, church, music videos, and the people around them—about sex and relationships that seemingly contradict what they see in mainstream media and what they are taught within the culture. These messages create relationship scripts that can be damaging to relationships if not modified. They often grow up believing they will have beautifully enriched connections with a man that will send them into the bliss of "happily ever after." The reality of this experience is different due to the embodiment of the social conditioning.

As a result, it's not surprising that studies indicate that Black women have three relationship scripts that shape their expectations around intimacy:

- Black women believe that Black men control relationships. Biblically, the man is depicted as the head of the household and that model is pervasive in many Black communities. So Black women go into a relationship believing they have no power, or even if they do think they have power, they lack the language and mentality to exert that power. In a relationship the perception of power or the perception of a lack of power can lead to dissension.

- Black women believe they are responsible for maintaining relationships. Even if it's the man in the relationship that is upset, it falls to the woman to figure out what is wrong and fix it. You can also see this in a principle saying that Black women are taught: "Drain your man before he leaves the house" (make sure your man is sexually satisfied). In both these scenarios, the man is absolved of all responsibility in figuring out how to improve or maintain the relationship. This attitude is often seen in situations where the woman has become the caregiver to their mate, children, parents, or other family members.

• Black women believe that male infidelity is normal and that Black men shouldn't be queried or punished for being sexually unfaithful. You know how many times I have heard someone say, "It's better to have a piece of a man than no man at all"? I stopped counting a long time ago.

These points make Black women enablers of Black men's misbehavior and mistreatment of Black women. These scripts make them grateful for whatever emotional attachment or commitment Black men show or bestow on their relationship. It also creates a narrative of diminished self-esteem and love.

The messages about sex tell the Black woman that the Black male understands intimacy only from a sexual relations perspective. For women who have been indoctrinated into a religious belief, pursuing intimacy with their partner through sex might pose a great challenge to intimacy. Research and diverse studies on sexuality have proven that men, regardless of race, view intimacy through the lens of sexual interaction with their partner. And since Black heterosexual women are often dependent on Black males to build intimacy (because in general they prefer a Black male partner), they would need to get accustomed to a Black male's understanding of intimacy or to sporadic conflicts with Black males on account of sexual incompatibility. Interestingly, we set ourselves up for this "truth" as a culture. We have been told that when we get married, we should just expect to stop having sex as often and expect to argue with our partner about our imperfections. And we should hush up about it because no one wants a nagging woman.

That's why we see two typical sexual scripts for Black women:

1. Black men control sexual encounters.
2. Black women do not really desire sex.

Black women's sexual scripts relating to control attest to the potential imbalance of power in the relationship. Psychologists conducted a qualitative study that captured Black women's thoughts about sexual intimacy. Although Black women wanted more physically intimate and monogamous relationships, they reported difficulties combating social norms that promote non-monogamy. Black women's tendency to script sexual intimacy along the lines of stereotypes made it possible for them to always expect an oversexed, unemotional attitude from Black men.

The study suggests some Black women have learned to integrate the possibility of infidelity and abusive relationship behaviors into their relational scripts. Thus, to get to a particular level of intimacy, they may use sex as a function of currency in exchange for emotional intimacy from their partners.[21] Intimacy

---

21 Eleanor McLellan-Lemal et al., "'A Man's Gonna Do What a Man Wants to Do': African American and Hispanic Women's Perceptions about Heterosexual Relationships: A Qualitative Study," *BMC Women's Health* 13, no. 1 (May 2013): 27, https://doi:10.1186/1472-6874-13-27.

cannot survive in such relationships. Often the connections sought are sabotaged by this script.

Black women's relationship scripts can certainly go beyond sexual expectations. Older women emphasize receiving economic support from men. Younger women talk more about the importance of emotional intimacy with their male partner. The historical and cultural messages about the roles of women vs. men, whether stated outright or implied by behavior, have led to a narrative where Black women feel and seek more connection with their partners with little reciprocation from Black men. The teaching of this narrative further alienates the Black female from the Black male.

Thus, before they even start a relationship, Black females already have a preconceived notion that Black males will dump their intimacy responsibilities on them.

The Relationship Scripts of Black Men

When compared to their female counterparts, literature regarding Black men's sex and relationship socialization is scarce. Some psychologists believe that Black men's experiences with their family of origin directly correlate to their attitudes and beliefs about romantic relationships.[22] These experiences include bullying, a combative nature, and rivalry between parents and between siblings. Hostile, harsh, and emotionally dismissive parenting during mid-adolescence has been shown to affect relationship behaviors in emerging adulthood.

---

22 Armon Rashard Perry, "African American Men's Attitudes Toward Marriage," *Journal of Black Studies* 44, no. 2 (March 2013): 182-202, https://doi:10.1177/0021934712472506.

Black men have been taught mainly to expect that "emotional female beings" need to be pacified in an effort to reach the
male goal of sex. By using money, a little time, gifts, or the idea
that "baby, you are the only one for me," Black men can have sex,
achieve the desired orgasms, and navigate life without being committed to one woman. Unfortunately, if a woman is not "putting
out" in the relationship, Black men were taught that they did not
really need to try to take care of them. Remember, during slavery,
a Black man's socialization was simply procreation. Until relatively
recently, Black men did not seek intimacy as I describe in this
book, and their lack of interest in or understanding of intimacy
has become a negative circle of dysfunctional intimacy. As a sign
of hope, however, whenever I mention the four types of intimacy,
a majority of my clients (including men) want to learn more. I get
excited when they ask. It lets me know they are truly interested
in making a change. That means future generations will benefit.

Other research on Black men's relationship scripts is
conflicting. It demonstrates that men experience competing
desires for emotional and sexual intimacy in their dating and
first sexual encounters with women.[23] In emerging adulthood,
men are often unsure of what they want first: to be in love or
to have sex. That's why an emerging adult heterosexual male
will believe that the relationship they have with a heterosexual
female happened because they fell in love. But in the true sense,
they wanted to have sex and they knew that falling in love was

23 David Wyatt Seal and Anke A. Ehrhardt, "Masculinity and Urban Men: Per-
    ceived Scripts for Courtship, Romantic, and Sexual Interactions with Women,"
    Culture, Health & Sexuality 5, no. 4 (July–August 2003): 295-319, https://
    doi:10.1080/136910501171698.

the easiest and most crime-free way to have sex. When a male develops with this orientation, they will often reconcile satisfying their sexual urge with falling in love. Thus, when their female partner refuses to surrender her body to them, they feel unloved, rejected, and unsuccessful at love. These negative feelings affect future intimacy.

I have learned over the years that the sexual pursuit and conquest of women tends to represent heterosexuality and masculinity for men in emerging adulthood.[24] For some, if sex occurs too early, it can impede developing emotional intimacy. They don't establish emotional intelligence through social-emotional learning and are not taught empathy for others; they think mostly in terms of their own immediate needs. Studies have proved that men who were sexually or emotionally abused in early or late childhood develop maladaptive sexual behavior.

Thus, most men with premature sexual or maladaptive emotional exposure often describe emotionally intimate relationships as scary and sexually limiting. Hence, they see the need to formulate reasons to explore emotional or sexual intimacy with multiple women. The result? The desire to seek sexual intimacy with a casual partner and emotional intimacy with non-sexual partners is heightened. This is often a manifestation of internalized conflictual messages about masculinity and male gender roles in most sexually and emotionally abused males.[25]

---

24 Antonia Randolph, "When Men Give Birth to Intimacy: The Case of Jay-Z's '4:44,'" *Journal of African American Studies* 22, no. 4 (December 2018): 393-406, https://doi:1o.1007/s12111-018-9418-4.

25 Kayla Charleston, "Act like a Lady, Think Like a Patriarch: Black Masculine Identity Formation within the Context of Romantic Relationships," *Journal of Black Studies* 45, no. 7 (October 2014): 660-678, https://doi:10.1177/0022193471454961.

CHANGING THE NARRATIVE

We tell ourselves that if we are going to be in a relationship with anyone, we won't and shouldn't repeat our mistakes. We also want to know that we are in a relationship with the right person, and, as such, we promise ourselves to accept only what's healthy for us. To make that happen, we have to change the scripts that play out in our minds. Here are three examples.

Janice is a PhD candidate and she realized one week that she would not be home as much as usual because she needed to work long hours to finish her dissertation. Her husband Robert wasn't happy about her workload, and under his old way of thinking would have criticized Janice for not making more time for him because she owed it to him as head of the household. But he has changed the script in his head so that now he looks for ways to understand and appreciate all of his wife's accomplishments without feeling any personal slight. Under this new way of thinking, he said to himself, "I have many things I can do while she is working. I am so proud of her." He then proceeded to spend time working on a new project at work, connect with two college friends who were in town, and organize a closet he fusses about each time he tries to find his tools. At the end of the week when Janice had completed the draft of her dissertation, she was eager to connect with her supportive husband.

Nancy grew up in a household where instability was the norm. She often felt unsafe, was rarely validated, and was told she would never amount to anything. She often felt abandoned in relationships because "[men] always seem to leave. I am just not worthy of anyone's time." When she and Michael began dating, she wanted to change the narrative and the outcome. So rather than sit back and wait for Michael to leave her then criticize him for his weak character (passive aggression), she decided to become assertive about her needs and desires. She told herself she *was* worthy of having a solid relationship and was honest with Michael about her history, saying to him, "I believe that you have my best interest at heart as I do yours. So, I will respond from a place of love and not out of fear that you will leave me." Saying that out loud to both herself and Michael has given their relationship a different, more positive path than what she has experienced in the past.

Antonio hated to be alone. He kept both a girlfriend and a "side chick" because he often felt lonely and bored. When one woman wasn't available, he could always go to the other. He was fully intimate with all of the women he dated. Fortunately, Antonio came to realize that feelings of loneliness and boredom are normal and they could be used for greater creativity if he tapped into their origin. After a few months of therapy, his internal narrative switched from "I have to find a woman to be with" to "how could I use this time to improve my life?" He began to spend time reading, watching documentaries, and investing in his personal growth. Antonio eventually learned to play golf and joined a regular team. His circle of friends, his profession, and his love interests changed. He acknowledged, "I did not know that having someone around kept me from knowing myself. I faced my issues and learned how to care for me. I don't even date the same. I like this space. I like me."

These stories we have in our heads about how intimacy should work and what we should expect of ourselves and others are very powerful. If you are struggling to achieve the intimacy you want, examine the narratives you are using. Are they holding you back? Are they influencing you to make choices that make intimacy harder to achieve rather than easier? Only you have the power to change the narratives that are influencing your behavior. Think about what is shaping your expectations and identify what you need to change your own inside-my-head stories so that you can achieve your intimacy goals.

CHAPTER 5

Below the Surface:
Recognizing the Importance of
Emotional and Mental Health

Years ago, a couple came to me with what may seem like familiar complaints. "Honestly," said Carson, the husband, "we are not having enough sex. I want more sex." Carson did not actually enjoy the intimacy of sex; he simply performed for his pleasure. He often left Sasha, his wife, unsatisfied. If she complained, he would become distant.

Sasha expressed a desire for more intimacy. She felt that even after five years of marriage, they did not know each other. "My husband says very little to me. We watch TV, eat dinners. I cook and pay our bills. The only time he really touches me is for sex."

Sasha said she often asked about Carson's childhood experiences, friendships, and girlfriends of his youth. Carson's response? "I never understood her desire to know so much. I do not want to talk about the past."

The husband wants physical intimacy. The wife wants to talk. Seems straightforward, right? But there was much more going on below the surface with this couple, as there is with most couples. In this case, past hurts and traumas were affecting Carson's and Sasha's emotional and mental health and were inhibiting their ability to become more intimate.

Far too often, mental and emotional health issues are kept in the shadows. And the truth is that until these issues can be brought into the light and dealt with openly, couples will struggle with intimacy. My goal in this chapter is to help make it easier for people to talk about issues of mental and emotional health by presenting a few basics. This is not meant to be a comprehensive discussion of mental health, but I hope it will open the door for couples to explore these issues.

WHAT CARSON WAS HIDING

Over the course of six months of weekly therapy, we discovered that Carson had tremendous anxiety and depression. Eventually, the reasons for these mental and emotional stressors became clear when Carson opened up and described how he had been sexually molested as a child. He was taken behind an abandoned building at six years old and made to perform oral sex on two adult men. At age twelve, his babysitter, also a male, sodomized him and taught Carson to do the same to his younger brother. Carson's sexual development and emotional understanding of love and affection were established in these experiences. He expressed feelings of shame, fright, disgust, and powerlessness over these early child-hood experiences. Eventually he confessed, "All I know is that cumming makes me feel like I did something right."

When Carson began having relationships with women as a teenager and later in his adult life, his experience taught him that sex was forceful and ended with the male orgasm; there was no connection to feelings of love, passion, desire, fulfill-ment, or affection. There was no positive introspection or quality decision-making present to assist him in building meaningful relationships. This seemed to work for Carson since none of his girlfriends complained openly.

It's perhaps no surprise that later in life when Carson dated Sasha, he was comfortable because she too said or did nothing that challenged his relationship script. Once they got married, however, she was dissatisfied with their sexual encounters. She attempted to talk with Carson about his experiences and what he found pleasing. Carson was not receptive to these conversa-tions because, unbeknownst to her, they brought up the pain of his abuse. Rather than talk about childhood experiences, Carson often told jokes or was slightly self-deprecating to dismiss her desire for knowledge.

Carson was ashamed of his sexual history. He was unwilling to open up and discuss what occurred, and though he was in ther-apy, he did not want to discuss these challenges. Often, in an effort to create a barrier he would use Biblical principles to describe his spouse's desires as ungodly. As long as it kept him from connect-ing emotionally, he was satisfied.

The lack of connection between the full range of emotions and his sexual experience was a normal and natural state of being for Carson, so he truly believed that he functioned as any man would during sex. In one session, he stated, "I know I am bringing the hammer and getting it in. No woman has complained until now." In a later session, he blurted out in anger: "This marriage thing got me struggling. Nobody else has complained."

Other factors arose the more Carson revealed about his upbringing. When he talked about how he was raised, he would discuss the lack of connection with his siblings, the sexual abuse he experienced at the hands of his uncle, the anger he felt toward his mother and stepmother, the distrust he had toward men in general, and the limited palate he developed due to the food insecurity. The more he revealed, the clearer it became that many of his behaviors toward Sasha were connected to his childhood trauma. Internally, Carson felt insecure but had no safe space to explore reconciling his frustrations.

For her part, though Sasha empathized with Carson's abuse, cried when she heard the details, and was eager to make him feel better, she had challenges understanding how Carson could associate sex with her to the horrific acts he had suffered as a child. It took some work for her to understand how to process and accept the ways in which Carson's past was affecting his present and, if he did nothing, his future.

While Carson's situation may be extreme, many of us in the Black community have negative experiences that are affecting our mental and emotional health. Unfortunately, in Black culture, discussions of mental health are extremely taboo. Y'all know we are quick to take it to the altar or "keep Uncle Joe in his room" (that is, keep a relative who is odd or has mental health challenges in a separate room rather than allow them to join the "normal" members of the family who are chatting in the living room or kitchen). Nobody knows what is happening with Uncle Joe or if it is hereditary because we will not discuss the details. We do not know our psychological history even though it is part of our medical history. Work on mental and emotional health—and healing our traumas, whether recent or buried in the distant past—is paramount to achieving deep intimacy with a partner. That work is best done with guidance from a licensed therapist or counselor.

EMOTION AND BRAIN FUNCTION: WHY OVERCOMING TRAUMA IS SO DIFFICULT

When people hear about Carson's story, one common reaction they have is that once he was able to acknowledge how his past traumas were affecting him, he should have been able to rationally control his behavior and start acting and thinking in new ways. Unfortunately, it's not that simple. And to explain why, we have to dig a little into brain anatomy and function and how it relates to our emotions.

The cognitive psychology of emotional intimacy attempts to solve the puzzles associated with traumatic memory, reasoning, judgment, and feelings. Sometimes we marvel at the prospect of remembering certain past events as if they just happened. At other times, we quickly forget recent memories. Or we might remember things differently than a friend or family member. There are even moments when a conversation sparks a memory and we are triggered by judging thoughts and reason why we made a particular decision. If the conversation taps an intense memory, we might become emotional and even express that emotion through body language or verbalize excitement and discomfort. This is attributed to our cognitive process and the emotions connected to the memory.

There are five parts of the brain that play a big role in determining how we process memories and the emotions they invoke. (See Figure 5.1.)

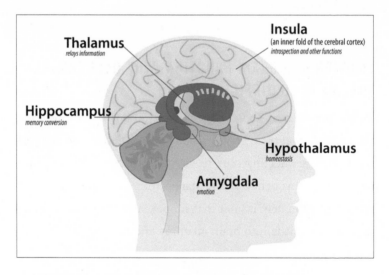

Figure 5.1: Parts of the brain involved in emotions and memories

1. Hippocampus: The hippocampus is the area that stores the memories associated with experiences we have had throughout life.

2. Amygdala: This area processes the emotions associated with the experiences stored in the hippocampus.

3. Insula: The insula is the a part of the brain that helps
   with introspection, our sense of balance, and our awareness of the location of feelings that exist in the body, as
   well as decision-making.

4. Thalamus: The thalamus is our center for self-regulation.
   This is where we work out conflicting and incongruent thoughts connected to the emotions residing in the
   amygdala.

5. Hypothalamus: This is the gland that seeks homeostasis
   to regulate involuntary functions like body temperature,
   breathing, heart rate, sex drive, and hunger in response to
   various stimuli in the aforementioned areas.

Now let's look at Carson's experiences again to understand
how they affected what went on in his brain:

- His memories of the molestation were storied in his
  hippocampus, and they influenced how he approached
  relationships as an adult.

- Whenever he thought about those experiences, the feelings
  of shame and powerlessness were triggered in his amygdala.
  Those memories had no connection to positive feelings of
  love, passion, desire, fulfillment, or affection.

- He had no reference for processing and reframing those
  negative emotions (hypothalamus dysregulation).

- There was no positive introspection and quality decision-
  making present in the insula to assist him in building
  meaningful relationships.

- Carson's physical reactions—the rapid pulse, sweating, etc.—were caused by his hypothalamus.

In other words, talking about anything that would bring up his memories triggered negative feelings and physical stress, with no mechanisms in his brain to stop the cascade. His brain went into overload, which prohibited him from making positive relationship connections whenever emotions were explored. Even knowing that this cascade would happen was not enough to stop it. That is, you can't rationalize your way out of the ingrained way your brain is processing and reacting to information.

That's why professional counseling or therapy is often helpful when dealing with traumatic or challenging experiences, whether from childhood or from present-day experiences. In therapy, couples can learn to provide safety in expression of both cognitive and emotional intimacy. These skills were not demonstrated, or, if demonstrated, not understood as necessary for a healthy marital relationship. They needed to actively do something different. Had Carson and Sasha continued for a few more years with their dysfunction, they likely would have divorced. The mental health concerns increased their challenges immensely.

ARE ANXIETY OR DEPRESSION AFFECTING YOUR RELATIONSHIPS?

If you work with a therapist, it's likely that one of the first steps they will take is evaluating whether anxiety or depression is affecting your everyday life and, in particular, your ability to develop intimacy in your relationships. According to the standard reference manual used by therapists and psychiatrists (DSM 5, or the Diagnostic and Statistical Manual of Mental Disorders Fifth Edition), "Fear is the emotional response to a real or perceived imminent threat, whereas anxiety is *anticipation* of a future threat."

Often, where there is intense anxiety, depression follows. They have similar symptoms so I speak of them together. I'll talk about Carson's specific symptoms in a bit but first, let's understand general anxiety disorders (GAD) better. The term GAD encompasses a wide range of conditions and severity where an individual's fear and anxiety controls their ability to function socially, which in turn creates instability in their behavior and dysfunction in their relationships.

In Black communities, GAD is common. We often see people who are accustomed to functioning with high levels of anxiety. They look good on the outside: dressed to the nines, wearing their Sunday best with a full face of makeup and the largest hat from their closet; at the party with crisp white sneakers without a crease at the toe. On the inside they are falling apart. They feel abnormal if their heart is not beating fast, if they *don't* feel the desire to run, if they aren't constantly looking for the other shoe to drop, if they aren't out somewhere looking for the "tea." They have a nauseous feeling in their gut. They feel anything good is too good to be true. They are angry and irritable. You can't ask them nothing or they'll snap your head off, always yelling, talking about "that's just how I sound." They look at you like they're waiting for the problem to start.

continued

"Bet not nobody" is how they start every sentence or they say, "If you loved me, you'd call me." Everything is "sus." Money is always funny, cause they will buss a cap. Need I go on?

I know, I know, you're thinking, "That's not me." Right? This is yo momma and them or Pookey and Bumpy or the neighbor, but it is certainly not you. Their normal state is a continual need to be on the defensive, to get assurances that everything is OK; they will often sweat profusely in crowded areas. Sometimes, even if unconsciously, they will create unnecessary drama.

Those who suffer from GAD seek comfort in various defense mechanisms and distance themselves from situations that have the potential to trigger an episode. The problem is that *anything* can trigger this anxiety. General anxiety disorder has the potential to manifest in various types of anxiety disorders. It does not always result in physical symptoms of distress; more often it appears in behaviors. For example, people who suffer from GAD have an overactive imagination when it comes to foreseeing potential disasters in everyday life events. They worry excessively about finances, work, family/marital relationships and well-being, household responsibilities, and their children well into adulthood. Many of these concerns occur simultaneously, causing great dysfunction in their ability to complete or stay focused on even menial tasks and especially on projects that require attention to detail. Those with GAD may become paralyzed in their decision-making and do nothing, which makes many situations worse. They may not be mentally or emotionally present in social environments or their relationships. They might be considered too sensitive in other areas of their relationship.

Those who are living with GAD worry about their sexual encounters and wonder if their performance is satisfactory, yet they rarely ask their partner's opinion. Why? They fear rejection.

General anxiety disorder clients are more likely to express difficulty in "social, occupational, or other important areas of functioning" (DSM 5, 2013). As a result, an employer, family member, or friend might refer the client to therapy. Through assessments (i.e., self-reporting, behavioral observation, structured interviews, and even personality inventories) a mental health therapist will be able to interpret additional symptoms of restlessness, fatigue, feelings of tension, sleep deprivation, irritability, and difficulty remembering simple details or concentrating. Therapists often find that GAD sufferers exhibit behaviors associated with other anxiety disorders and depression. Overall, GAD has longevity and occurs frequently at varying levels in a client's history.

Evaluating Anxiety and Depression

As a first step in evaluating anxiety and depression, a therapist or counselor will ask a client to rate themselves on how often they have certain feelings or exhibit certain behaviors. You can see the evaluation forms in Table 5.1 (GAD) and Table 5.2 (Depression). In both cases, the person marks the answers for each criteria, then adds up the scores. The total ratings indicate whether the condition is severe and/or frequent, as indicated in the scoring tables below each figure.

Over the <u>last 2 weeks</u>, how often have you been bothered by the following problems?	Not at all	Several days	More than half the days	Nearly every day
1. Feeling nervous, anxious or on edge	0	1	2	3
2. Not being able to stop or control worrying	0	1	2	3
3. Worrying too much about different things	0	1	2	3
4. Trouble relaxing	0	1	2	3
5. Being so restless that it is hard to sit still	0	1	2	3
6. Becoming easily annoyed or irritable	0	1	2	3
7. Feeling afraid as if something awful might happen	0	1	2	3

Total Score _____ = Add Columns _____ + _____ + _____

GAD Score	Severity of Anxiety
0-4	Mild
5-9	Moderate
10-14	Moderately Severe
15-21	Severe

If you checked off <u>any</u> problems, how <u>difficult</u> have these problems made it for you to do your work, take care of things at home, or get along with other people?

Not difficult at all	Somewhat difficult	Very difficult	Extremely difficult
☐	☐	☐	☐

Table 5.1 General Anxiety Disorder Evaluation & Scoring

Over the last 2 weeks, how often have you been bothered by the following problems?	Not at all	Several days	More than half the days	Nearly every day
1. Little interest or pleasure in doing things	0	1	2	3
2. Feeling down, depressed, or hopeless	0	1	2	3
3. Trouble falling or staying asleep, or sleeping too much	0	1	2	3
4. Feeling tired or having little energy	0	1	2	3
5. Poor appetite or overeating	0	1	2	3
6. Feeling bad about yourself, that you are a failure, or have let yourself or your family down	0	1	2	3
7. Trouble concentrating on things, such as reading the newspaper or watching television	0	1	2	3
8. Moving or speaking so slowly that other people could have noticed? Or the opposite—being so fidgety or restless that you have been moving around a lot more than usual	0	1	2	3
9. Thoughts that you would be better off dead or of hurting yourself in some way	0	1	2	3

Total Score _____ = Add Columns _____ + _____ + _____

Depression Score	Severity of Depression
0-4	None or Minimal
5-9	Mild
10-14	Moderate
15-21	Moderately Severe
20-27	Severe

Table 5.2. Depression Evaluation & Scoring

With depression in particular, therapists are trained to look beyond these self-scored indicators. Most people think that individuals with depression are openly sad and distressed. They lack energy to do anything, and their homes are a mess. These symptoms may show up, but I have found that in the Black community there are a few others that are depression cover-ups. In my experience, I've seen the following behaviors used to mask depression:

- Dressing to the nines. Now we do this as a people in general; however, those with depression must be impeccable for public consumption. Even their cars are kept nearly spotless.

- Shopping excessively. Often, there is no money for these excursions. They are "retail therapy."

- Being a social butterfly. These people call everyone friend.

- Maintaining distance in relationships. These people have transactional relationships, where any interactions are kept superficial. They do not see these people as friends; the "friends" know very little about the depressed individual.

- Being a busy-body. These folks know everyone's business.

Now, hear me when I say not everyone exhibiting these behaviors is depressed. Consult a therapist to be sure. And . . . do not take this list to your family and try to diagnose them. My point is that depression can appear in many different disguises, so just because someone isn't sitting around crying all day, don't assume they are *not* depressed.

WORKING THROUGH ANXIETY AND DEPRESSION: CARSON AND SASHA'S EXPERIENCE

When Sasha talked about her dissatisfaction with their relationship, Carson's internal physical signs of distress were obvious to him only: increased heart rate, racing thoughts, sweaty palms, difficulty concentrating, and shallow breathing. His behaviors, however, were palpable according to Sasha. "He immediately speaks to me with a raised voice, sharp tone, and dismissiveness when we're alone," she said.

Carson's GAD assessment revealed that he experienced anxiety symptoms consistently across all seven categories (score of 18 out of a maximum 21 points, falling into the "severe" category). This made it very difficult for him to do work, take care of things at home, or get along with people. Carson was inattentive to his wife, but sought affirmation from other friends and family. Carson had immense difficulty staying at home or connecting with his children in meaningful ways. He often thought people were "out to get [him]. They are all coming for [him] in one way or another."

Carson's depression score was a 15 out of 27 (in the "moderately severe" category). The depression intensified Carson's condition. There were intense moments when he snapped at Sasha and the children. "[He did it] in a soft tone that was eerily combative," Sasha said. "It left you feeling diminished and unworthy, unloved, and stupid." Carson competed with everyone.

The result of these assessments were very difficult for Carson and Sasha to accept. They both grew up in religious environments and communities that did not believe in anxiety or depression. Sasha said that she saw Carson interact with others around them, exchanging depth of thought, perspective, and intimate conversation. She did not comprehend his "selective anxiety." She said, "Certainly he wasn't depressed. He is a social butterfly."

They allowed me to offer a weekly treatment plan that included talk therapy and medication. Carson began to feel a difference in his physiological signs within four weeks. Sasha began to see a difference in Carson's cognitive intimacy (his willingness to share thoughts and ideas). He was more present and in the moment, listening to conversations, clarifying his understanding, and offering relative perspectives. Eventually, emotional connections began developing as well.

Sasha completed the assessments and discovered she too was exhibiting signs of depression. She began to question her beliefs around relationships and why she was so accepting of Carson's behaviors.

Each of them began to establish new habits for pointing out triggers and discussing them in an emotionally safe environment. When they began to say things that were hurtful, they took a break but always set a time for returning to the conversation so that nothing was allowed to fester or remain unaddressed.

Cognitive intimacy relates to emotional intimacy in that it requires conflict resolution and collaboration with your partner. It means you will take the time to stretch your emotional response beyond your immediate feelings, process them honestly with your partner, and allow the cognitive intellect to embrace the authenticity of those feelings. Emotional intimacy is sharing the ways in which your experiences shape your decision-making, judgment, reasoning, and emotional connection to life's challenges and success. When cognitive distortions exist in the emotional process, you will shut down, dismiss your partner's perspective and feelings, jump to conclusions, minimize the significance of an issue, "catastrophize" experiences that are not at all connected to the situation or relationship and, above all, personalize everything.

Cognitive and emotional intimacy are instrumental for focus, understanding and expression, and synthesizing and integrating information. They are also responsible for encoding, storing, and retrieving information as well as utilizing the perceived information to solve problems. Thought, as a cognitive process, deals with higher emotional reasoning. The sort of emotionality in reasoning is what we need to solve our intimacy problems. Carson and Sasha saw the need for cognitive and emotional intimacy to solve other problem areas.

TAKING CARE OF YOUR OWN MENTAL HEALTH

If you are diagnosed with a mental health disorder (clinical depression, personality disorder, etc.), you will have to do some work on your own with professionals so you learn how to cope with the condition and can decide on what treatments (if any) are best for you.

If your partner is diagnosed with a mental health disorder, recognize that you may not be able to help them. And, as the flight attendants always remind us, you should "put on your own oxygen mask first before assisting someone else."

In either case, recognize that you may need to step away from your partner—either temporarily or permanently—while you both deal with

continued

the situation. Your primary responsibility is to make sure you are safe and taking care of your own mental health, even if that means you must abandon your current relationship.

COMING INTO THE LIGHT

Intimacy takes courage. And nowhere is that more evident than when it comes to our emotional and mental health. Only by having the courage to deal with these issues and ensuring that we are actively working to improve our emotional and mental health will we be able to trust that our future with our partners will not repeat patterns of the past.

As I said at the beginning of this chapter, my intent here was not to provide a comprehensive guide to emotional and mental health challenges that can prevent true intimacy. Rather, my hope is to make it easier and more acceptable for Black couples to talk about topics like these. And if you read something that resonates with your own experiences as an individual or couple, then I encourage you to seek out professional help.

Now listen, I know not all therapists are equipped to handle Black cultural dynamics, nor do they always relate to the challenges we deal with by way of the skin we are in. But all skin folk ain't kinfolk, and cultural competency isn't easy. So just like you go try out a barber or hairstylist or a few churches in a new town, you need to seek the right fit for your therapy. Do not give up. You know the song . . . Try therapy, it's all right. I done tried it and it's all right.

CHAPTER 6

How We Bond with Others

Not everything that is faced can be changed, but
nothing can be changed until it is faced.

—James Baldwin

Whether or not you've suffered traumas like Carson or
had a much less turbulent and stable upbringing like
Sasha, the person you are today, and how you react
and behave, is shaped in large part by the experiences of your
childhood. That's why another important area in understanding our emotional and mental health is understanding that
those experiences have shaped how we approach relationships
in adulthood.

The term that psychologists use for this area of study is
"attachment," although "bonding" is a more common term
among laypeople. The study of attachment explores how easy or
difficult it is for people to become emotionally connected with

others, which has a huge impact on their ability to become intimate, as you'll see in this chapter.

ATTACHMENT STYLES

Attachment was first studied in infants by British psychologists
John Bowlby and Mary Ainsworth. The basic premise was that
no parent is dependable and available all the time. Bowlby and
Ainsworth were able to observe that infants demonstrate distress
and fear when they are separated from their parents. According
to Bowlby and Ainsworth's study, infants are essentially asking
themselves three questions:

- Is the attachment figure nearby?
- Are they accessible?
- Are they attentive?

If the infant's perception of the answers is yes, they become
overwhelmed with love, confidence, and have a feeling of security. When left alone, these infants do all they can to search for
their parents: cry, turn in the direction of the parent, or crawl to
the door the parent exited. Then they are comforted upon the
parent's return. As children, they are more inclined to explore
their environment, play with others, and be generally sociable
because they believe they are safe. When they reach adulthood,
these children are less likely to fly off the handle or overreact to
negative emotions; they find it easier to return positive emotions; they are confident and resilient.

If the infant's perception of the answers is no—that is, the person they want to be close to is not nearby and/or pays them little attention—they will develop anxious feelings such as isolation, ambiguity, emotional distance, dramatic disposition, and internal conflict. If line-of-sight (physical proximity) and emotional connections are not restored quickly, the infant's desire for the parent can wane. Eventually, it seems that these children neither want to prevent a separation from their parents nor do they want to *re-establish* proximity when the parent returns. This seems to be a coping skill that prepares them for future pain. As adults, this experience of despair is demonstrated in turbulent relationships, imagined bonds with potential partners, and attention seeking. They will develop a coping skill that will shield them from future hurt and pain and often subconsciously place them in direct conflict with avoiding that same discomfort.

Ultimately, Ainsworth developed descriptions of four kinds of attachment styles common in children, as shown in Figure 6.1:

- Secure
- Anxious-Preoccupied
- Fearful-Avoidant[26]
- Dismissive-Avoidant

---

26 R. Chris Fraley, "Adult Attachment Theory and Research: A Brief Overview," http://labs.psychology.illinois.edu/~rcfraley/attachment.htm.

SECURE	ANXIOUS-PREOCCUPIED
Confident Reciprocal Non-reactive Resilient	Emotional hunger Fantasy bond Lack of nurturing Turbulent
DISMISSIVE-AVOIDANT	FEARFUL-AVOIDANT
Isolation Ambiguity Ambivalence Emotionally distant	Internal conflict Dramatic Unpredictable Ambivalence

Figure 6.1. Characteristics of the Four Attachment Styles

A LEGACY OF UNHEALTHY ATTACHMENTS

In a previous chapter, I talked about the legacy of slavery and the harm it did to the development of healthy intimate relationships between Black men and women. So, long before Bowlby and Ainsworth even began studying the phenomenon of attachment styles, Black people were living with attachment challenges day in and day out. The enmity between Black men and women continued after slavery-era systems built to effectively challenge our ability to become more stable because society did not desire that we exist among them. Thus, the racial discrimination Black men and women face has affected our ability to build the kind of secure attachments that are necessary for healthy intimate relationships.

YOUR EMOTIONAL BONDS WITH A PARTNER REFLECT THOSE OF YOUR PARENTS

The nature of the relationship between infant-attachment figures is apparent throughout human development. According to researchers Hazan and Shazer, the emotional bond that develops between adult romantic partners is partly a function of the bond that was formed between an infant and their attachment figure. They were able to establish that there are similar features in the attachment pattern between infant-attachment figures and adult partners in a romantic relationship. Both infants and their caretakers and adult romantic partners—

1. Feel safe when their attachment figure is nearby and accessible.

2. Favor intimate, bodily contact over long-distance communication.

3. Feel anxious, desperate, depressed, and insecure when their attachment figure is unavailable or inaccessible.

4. Develop negative coping skills and defense mechanisms to prevent future hurt.

In short, the experiences we have as infants, and how we connected or not with our parents or caretakers, have a huge impact on if and how we bond with our adult romantic partners. If our relationship with our parent as an infant was anxious, dismissive, or avoidant, we will likely become needy, withdrawn, or detached in adulthood.

With corrective measures, generally in therapy, these attachment disorders can be reversed. An example of this is Rebecca,
who came to see me after experiencing a very painful break-up
in her late 20s with a partner she'd been with more than a year.
In therapy, she discovered that the way she handled emotional
hurt was impacting, to a great extent, how she was relating with
each new partner. She attempted to protect or preserve her feelings and finances by erecting emotional barriers. She told me
that when she and her most recent partner went on vacation,
she always split the bills fifty-fifty. She had trouble thinking of
herself as being part of a couple and still spoke of events using
"I statements" vs. "we statements," even as the couple discussed
their future.

Rebecca was acting out of a fear-avoidant attachment style.
She thought she was preserving her emotions by removing
expectations and ensuring her own security. Her partner desired
a deeper connection that allowed them to plan a future together.
He eventually became frustrated and ended the relationship.

Avoiding confrontations and shielding the heart from pain is
a survival skill that can limit intimacy and prevent the strengthen-
ing of the emotional bond between partners. Neither a clingy nor
a withdrawn individual can build healthy intimacy with a partner. The prevailing reality of Black-couple marriages is that many
children grow up in single-parent homes. While many parents
have been able to build resilience in their children, the single-
parent-household phenomenon is bound to create instances of
resentment and detachment between child and parent.

Sometimes, out of necessity, the parent has to work more
than one job or work later hours or allow the village to carry

greater responsibility for parenting. The parent might not have the emotional fortitude for expressing love beyond correction and fear for the safety of their child. It does not mean that healthy, intimate relationships are impossible to Black couples. It does mean that they must have a greater understanding of the internal and external cultural dynamics that make the work of Black Love more tedious. We desire the goal of greater intimacy and work is required to ensure longevity of the relationship.

A secure, emotional adult is more forthcoming with emotions. They will be able to seek support from their romantic partner and also reciprocate an equal measure of support. Adults with a secure attachment style will be able to experience a more integrative sense of self because they can understand themselves and intimacy on all of the four levels discussed in chapter 7: cognitively, emotionally, spiritually, and physically. They can compromise and make healthy choices about their needs, wants, and desires within the relationship. They do not have great difficulty with boundaries or consequences. Secure adults understand the need for the individuality of the couple. They will be open to positive changes and options for growth. An adult with a secure attachment is more likely to have a longer and more stable relationship.

Another client, Noel, was the second child in a family of three children and divorced parents. She said that her parents had separated when she was fourteen months old and had gotten divorced when she was five. Her father never asked for custody. Before her parents separated, her mother was pregnant with her younger brother. After the separation, her elder sister was sent to live with an aunt while she was left in the care of her maternal grandmother, Gram, which turned out to be less than ideal. In addition to Gram, Noel was living with four older cousins, a few uncles, and an aunt. The family was always bickering. Whenever problems arose, Gram blamed the parents of each of the children, she blamed the children, she blamed the government, and she blamed God for "the burden of raising these kids and having deadbeat children." They had food scarcity. The male cousins were incestuous. The aunts were constantly angry with their boyfriends. The uncles could not keep jobs. Gram spoke of them as if they were the cross she had to bear to qualify for heavenly paradise. Noel spent ten years of her life living in these conditions.

As an adult, Noel had difficulty forming healthy attachments. She believed that she would be abandoned. "I would ask myself, what if they leave me. Then I would start fights so we could break up." Noel did not believe she was worthy of love. She spoke with a raised voice in every conversation and welcomed confrontation. "I am not going to allow anyone to mess around with my life anymore," she said.

Noel is just like many who developed attachment disorders in their youth. They fear abandonment, have separation anxiety, are withdrawn in relationships, have control issues, have difficulty managing their anger, and are often impulsive. These reactions to the trauma they experienced in childhood become survival skills as adults.

LEAVING THE BAGGAGE BEHIND

We all enter into relationships with assumptions, experiences, and our truth. The last two factors—experiences and

truth—might help us make quality decisions and foster intimacy in our relationships. But assumptions exist mostly to
ruin intimacy before it is established. Assumptions are defined
by "what-ifs." The numerous what-ifs arising from emotional
instability have ruined many promising relationships. It is the
what-ifs that cause many couples to unintentionally sabotage
their ability to build genuine intimacy with their partner.

Fearing a thing will happen or fearing the outcome
of something that has happened is a valid emotion. We are
entitled to our fears. If you are in a committed romantic relationship with someone, you are responsible for ensuring you
have a healthy attachment style. While it is true that some
fears from past experiences exist to point us in the right direction, these same fears, when allowed to roam unchecked, are
capable of affecting intimacy in our relationships. We cannot
allow those fears and attachment disorders to disable our ability to create meaningful relationships.

When I was working with one couple, the husband, Marcus,
expressed his fear of abandonment and acknowledged that he
was cheating on his wife in an effort to reassure himself that
he would always be in a relationship. His wife initially was irate
and defensive at the idea of his cheating. When she was able to
focus on his emotional safety and hear the fear that underlay
his behavior, the couple began the conversation about how to
make Marcus feel more secure in their relationship. They then
began the process of building a trusting relationship by removing
defensiveness, criticism, silent treatment, and judgment.

Marcus also decided to receive individual therapy and discovered that his childhood led him to develop an unhealthy

concept of how to bond with other people. His attachment style was hindering his ability to love both himself and others. The work Marcus did to challenge his beliefs about self-worth transformed his ability to love his wife with greater freedom of expression. They grew emotionally, cognitively, and spiritually. This enhanced their physical sexual connection, and they learned to have more frequent spontaneous encounters.

Many of us are unaware of the ways in which our mental and emotional issues are holding us back. Anxiety and depression, or any other mental health challenges, may be leading us to behave in ways that are driving our partners away from us rather than bringing them closer to us.

We also all have experiences from childhood that may be affecting how we interact today, often for the worse instead of for the better. We may have fear or distrust in attachment. Imagine a small voice in your spirit . . .

1. That tells you that letting go means exposing your vulnerability. You are afraid of what will become of you if you should let your guard down. You hold on to the fear because you don't want your partner to see you too deeply.

2. That tells you that the reason for the fear could be repeated. Thus, you should always be on the lookout for signs of the offense. Most times, fear is linked to hurt and shame. It could be the shame of rejection, the shame of abandonment, shame of being, or shame of having been humiliated, or it could be the shame of betrayal. Hence, you are afraid of something. But what something?

3. That tells you to activate or rewrite your attachment pattern. In childhood, every human forms a pattern of attachment concerning beliefs, perceptions, and behaviors through experiences. Being that this pattern helped you to identify and regulate your emotions, even as far back as infancy, the experiences that come from your attachment pattern often affect or impact your functioning in the future.

Attachment is a vital part of intimacy. We can't rewrite our childhood or the ways it shaped our attachment style to suit the sort of adult experiences we desire. But we can acknowledge the truth of our past and recognize how it has shaped our behavior, for better or worse. And if it's for "the worse," then we can consciously work to make sure those early experiences do not prevent us from achieving our relationship goals today and into the future.

CHAPTER 7

Building a Foundation for Healthy Intimacy

To grow in our ability to love ourselves,
we need to receive love as well.

—John Gray

You can't have a secure, stable building unless you have a solid foundation. The same is true when it comes to intimacy: you can't create strong, lasting, intimate relationships unless you work at creating a strong foundation. Conversely, when the foundation of a structure is faulty, the structure will eventually fail.

In this chapter, I want to give you a model for how the many elements we've talked about in the book come together to build a strong foundation for healthy intimacy, and the key role that open and honest communication plays. This might

even involve inspecting childhood experiences that have created gaping cracks in your foundation. Remember, very early
in our development we begin to formulate attachment styles.
Trust me, unhealed emotional, mental, and physical trauma
from childhood will impact adult relationships whether romantic or platonic.

THE HIERARCHY OF NEEDS

In the 1940s, American psychologist Abraham Maslow was
studying human motivation: what shapes the choices that people make every day. The result of his research is a model that we
know today as Maslow's Hierarchy of Needs. The idea behind
his model is that all of us as human beings have a wide variety
of needs, ranging from the basics (such as food and water) to
the more esoteric (such as connection and fulfillment). Maslow
discovered that these needs function like the levels of a pyramid: you can't truly graduate to the second level until you
have mastered the first level, and so on. The ideas embedded
in the hierarchy also apply to building intimacy, so let's look at
Maslow's categories then see how they relate to intimacy.

THE FIVE LEVELS OF HUMAN NEEDS

Maslow's hierarchy has five levels of human needs grouped into
three categories, as shown in Figure 7.1: Let's look at them
starting from the bottom.

Figure 7.1: Maslow's Hierarchy of Human Needs

- Physiological Needs: These are the needs that keep us alive. This level includes our need for things like food, water, shelter, clothing, and sleep. The physiological needs form the base of the pyramid because if they are not met, the person will spend all of their attention focused on meeting them, rendering them unable to pay attention to anything else. An example of lack in this area is seen in poverty. Those who are impoverished often spend immense time attempting to fulfill their basic needs— constantly thinking about where the next meal, shelter, or clothing will come from. (Do you see the direct connection to the next level, safety?)

- Safety Needs: Safety is in the basic category because it encompasses employment, health, and security, the things that make us feel both physically safe and psychologically safe not just today but also as we think about the future. Having a place to stay, a place to store food, and a place to sleep is so important. I think we all agree with that. Being able to lock the front door on our residence allows us to feel like we can protect our family and possessions and keep ourselves out of danger, providing an extra layer of peace and stability. Employment clearly impacts whether our physiological needs are met. If a job does not provide adequate stability, people can be tempted to perform criminal activities to sustain their mere existence.

- Love and Belonging: Once we have met our basic needs, the stability created allows us to focus on making connections with other human beings. We want to feel as if we belong to a group, whether that be with a single partner, a small family, or a large group of friends. Even introverts desire and seek out love and acceptance. As humans we will work on building trust with a community. Sometimes, we will even go outside our immediate community if we are unable to secure a sense of love and belonging within. We essentially create a social ecosystem of friends, colleagues, and neighbors that fortifies the ideals established in the basic needs of the pyramid.

- Esteem: This level within the hierarchy is both internal and external. Internally, it is our ability to see ourselves as worthy and deserving of good. Good is determined by the individual and can be very abstract. The point is that we see ourselves through a positive lens: trustworthy, lovable, significant, intelligent, honest, capable, etc. Externally, this level involves how others see us and our efforts to earn their respect. Generally, those in the love and belonging phase develop a healthy sense of respect for us. We want our partners to recognize our achievements and see our perseverance as admirable.

- Self-Actualization: This top level is where we begin experiencing the culmination of our work as we develop a sense of accomplishment so we can respect ourselves. Confidence is increased through our achievements. Resilience is built by overcoming obstacles. At a higher level, awards or accolades from our peers may be bestowed. Self-actualization creates a greater sense of fulfillment in our lives.

These five levels are often divided into three categories, as shown in Figure 7.2:

- The lowest two levels are considered basic needs, what we need in order to physically survive.
- The middle two levels represent psychological needs, how we address our mental health and sense of well-being.
- The top level is labeled self-fulfillment, what happens when we achieve our full potential.

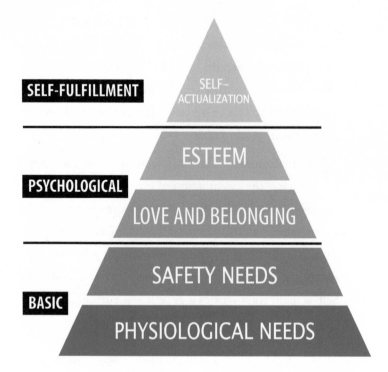

Figure 7.2. Categories of Need

THE HIERARCHY AND INTIMACY

When describing the levels of Maslow's Hierarchy, the path towards self-fulfillment may sound simple. Well, it ain't. As with any process with steps and a vertical trajectory, such as with a pyramid, we can climb up through intentional effort and slide down through simple missteps. This is a multi-layered, multi-faceted perspective on the complexity of life. And it can be utilized to feed the understanding of intimacy in much the same way.

When applying the hierarchy to intimate relationships, it's helpful to use slightly different labels, as shown in Figure 7.3:

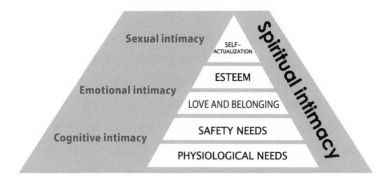

Figure 7.3: Intimacy and the Hierarchy of Needs

1. Spiritual Intimacy—Foundation of It All

Though spirituality was not specifically called out by Maslow, as I talked about in chapter 1, spirituality is the foundation of any relationship. I do not speak only of religion. I mean the core belief system that forms the crux of who you are as a person. It is in this spiritual core belief that we form our emotional, cognitive, and sexual understanding of the relationship scripts we govern our lives by. This concept forms the foundation of every relationship. The possibility of having a loving, committed, exciting, and connected intimacy with our partner depends on how solid and reliable we make the foundation of spirituality.

Why do I say that? Because everything starts in the spirit realm before it becomes tangible. This includes our relationships. We are spirit. Yes, we live in a physical body, but our experience of life starts in our minds and souls, conjuring up hopes, dreams, and desires. As partners help each other make those desires come to life, they are granted a very spiritual connection.

You and your partner were drawn to each other by your spirits. Trust me, a beautiful person with an ugly spirit becomes unattractive very quickly. So, though we first see with our physical eyes, we truly experience with our spirit. It provides the platform for the hierarchy as you discuss your beliefs and values, knowing they have and will shift, change, and morph over the years. Spiritual intimacy lives vibrantly when we live authentically in life and relationships. In the spiritual realm, you remove the mask and reveal yourself without fear of rejection.

Many relationships can be revitalized when they renew the spirit of the connection. Both partners, however, must be willing in each component of intimacy, and there is none like the commitment to spiritual intimacy. It engulfs the relationship and holds the understanding for the cognitive, emotional, and physical manifestation of who you become as one—a couple.

2. Cognitive Intimacy—Basic Needs (Physiological)

The basic need when it comes to intimacy concerns is problem-solving. Couples should be committed to solving the physical and emotional needs of the relationship. In chapter 1, I talked about how cognitive intimacy controls our ability to fulfill the other intimacy needs. Cognitive intimacy demands that importance be placed on understanding what is meant by food, shelter, clothing, and how these beliefs formed. It is the ability to have conversations of depth that challenge the intellect to grow beyond the basic and understand the intricate details of life.

Remember, cognitive intimacy provides a platform for a couple to explore each partner's history. Differences in socio-economic upbringing can create challenges in recognizing the basic need for steak as part of a meal versus hamburger helper. Yes, I'm breaking it down just like that! If one partner grew up not ever having eaten hamburger helper or not having eaten government cheese but that's what the other partner experienced, the way they shop in a grocery store, cook meals, and understand budgeting for the family could look different. Or, if one partner grew up putting a priority on experiences (living for the now) versus financial stability and the other partner grew up with the opposite attitude, one person could be considering how to set aside money for retirement while the other is looking for the next airline ticket so they can go zip-lining in Costa Rica. Simply put, this means that partners will need to consider how they adjust their lifestyle to accommodate the physiological needs of each other and ultimately the relationship.

3. Emotional Intimacy—Psychological Needs (Safety)

This is a crucial area. The psychological needs for safety include both physical safety and emotional safety. Can there be an opportunity to be open and honest without judgment? Is there a safe place to land so you can reveal your innermost secrets to your partner? Discussing insecurities about abandonment, resentment about becoming a parent, how to set boundaries, feelings about being unappreciated, or making decisions about money can be emotionally charged. It is important to set aside judgment and listen to understand each other, recognizing that jumping to conclusions or making assumptions could derail the ability to truly connect. To have an exciting and satisfying sexual encounter, each person needs to be comfortable with how they meet the needs of their partner in this area.

Emotional safety means that no matter the circumstances, both partners' perspectives are validated. Now, this does not mean you agree with everything that is said or done. It simply means that you acknowledge how they feel and recognize it as their truth. This is likely one of the most difficult commitments to the relationship. For instance, if a partner doesn't approve of a certain sexual adventure (threesomes, public acts, spanking, etc.), for the sake of maintaining their partner's self-esteem and interest, the other partner should be sensitive enough to not demand that adventure from their partner.

Couples should be emotionally alert (intelligent) to the emotional needs of their partners. Emotional alertness creates a sense of positive belongingness. And from belonging to each other, you will fulfill the intimacy needs of your partner. If you find yourself laughing or scoffing, making faces or closing yourself off to your partner's emotions, you will likely miss out on truly satisfying sexual explosions of ecstasy—I ain't just talking orgasms.

4. Sexual Intimacy—Self-Fulfillment Needs

The ultimate experience in a relationship is the physical, sexual exploration of two individuals that have connected beyond the penis and vagina. Yes. I said it. It is not about the act itself as much as it is the connection. That's the essence of HBNS (Hot Butt Naked Sex). It is in this phase that all the work accomplished in the cognitive, emotional, and spiritual space culminates into a song of pleasure, satisfaction, and joy. Here, couples aim to understand their sexual needs and then utilize these needs in achieving their full potential by engaging in creative sexual activities. This couple has self-actualized.

RECAP: THE HIERARCHY OF INTIMACY

- Cognitive intimacy means being able to have a mature, effective, healthy conversation about your likes and dislikes, childhood experiences, expectations, beliefs and values, what brings you pleasure or makes you happy—your physiological and safety needs. Making sure these needs are addressed allows for an increase of endorphins to move you toward deeper connection.

- It becomes possible to experience safety in being more vulnerable and open to express feelings of introspection that promote social growth (emotional intimacy). You can begin the process of feeling like you actually belong to a loving and caring partnership that is open to healthy communication and where your partner highly values your hopes, dreams, and desires. In this emotional phase, your partner can be open to understanding your feelings and how they impact the relationship overall.

- This allows you to move into a deeper connection with physical desire or sexual intimacy. And all of these connections are built within your spiritual intimacy, your shared beliefs, and your values. Let's dig a little deeper on how all these aspects of need relate to intimacy:

Making Connections at All Levels

While I've described this sequence as linear in its perspective, in reality there is seldom a linear path up the hierarchy. You are more likely to take a circuitous route, tackling issues in a different order or revisiting a lower level even if you have started work at the top levels. For example, as things change in the relationship there may be a need to reassess competence in any area of the relationship, so you may end up working on all three levels at once, or going back to revisit specific issues on a given level. The greatest challenge sometimes is removing judgment and being open to new perspectives as you enhance or re-build a relationship or forge a new one.

COMMUNICATION

What kept me sane was knowing that things would change, and it was the question of keeping myself together until they did.
—Nina Simone

I consider healthy communication to be another component of the foundation for healthy relationships. Effectively communicating your thoughts, ideas, and concerns to your partner is crucial to a healthy intimate relationship. Being able to regulate your emotions, not take things personally, jump to conclusions, or make assumptions is just as important on the listeners, end of the communication. Most couples, married, divorced or co-habitating, will attest to the importance of healthy, effective communication. No matter the culture, there is no substitution for effective, honest, positive communication. Notice how I keep adding adjectives to communication. I will take it a step further and say healthy, effective, honest, positive, affirming, and validating communication. When there is safety in communication, it is easier to perform each adjective without hesitation.

If one or both partners hesitate to communicate on the issues related to intimacy, that tells me the partner does not feel heard and feels misunderstood. If the body language and tone of voice indicates irritation rather than acceptance, empathy, validation, or affection, the person is not being open to their partner and probably not being open and honest about their own feelings and reactions. They might even be embarrassed by what they think or believe. Hesitation exists when egos do not desire to admit a lack of knowledge, when a partner feels controlled or out of control, when one partner exhibits the need to have the last word, no matter the conversation, "Houston, we have a problem."

You've seen the scenarios where secrets between partners—a lack of communication—lead to destruction of the relationship. For example, we've all seen couples that hide their financial challenges not just in the presence of friends and colleagues but from each other. A husband may sow a seed in the pastor's life without discussing the intentions with his spouse. Maybe he believes his spouse will disagree. Meanwhile, the wife charges dinner for a group of 20 friends on the corporate business card because her own card is maxed out. She rationalizes that she will figure it out later—but then the accounting department wants an expense report before payday and her misdeed is uncovered. Now, there is the potential for the husband to get fired for misuse of company funds. The husband might snap at his spouse in front of others to show dominance because at home he feels he has no power. Maybe she tells the children they can go to the movies and withdraws $40 from the ATM without mentioning it to her husband. Her girlfriends say, "You make money and contribute to the family. Why can't you make withdrawals when you want to?" With all the overdraft fees, they now pay $120, versus the $40 it actually costs, for a night of entertainment. Instead of communicating the issues with their spouse the husband takes advice from his barber, to "rob Peter to pay Paul."

I chose financial examples here, but the lack of communication could be about anything: children, sex, household responsibilities, spiritual matters. No matter the topic, many interactions between spouses are riddled with emotions tied to experiences, perspectives, and fears, real or imagined. Allowing the underlying issues to prevent open, honest, and vulnerable communication depletes opportunities to have intimate moments.

In each situation, the decision maker could have discussed their desires with their spouse. As a team they could have agreed on what to trust God with when sowing a seed into the pastor's life. They could have saved money for taking friends out for dinner. Better yet, if children witness their parents openly discussing issues such as how to access funding for a night of entertainment, it provides them with a model of healthy, effective, positive communication. All moments to build on cognitive, emotional, and even spiritual intimacy across generations.

Turning Arguments into Discussions: Keeping a Fight Fair

One of the quickest ways to derail communication is for a discussion to turn into an argument or fight. As part of a healthy,

intimate relationship, couples need to know how to have difficult discussions. Here are some rules for having a fair fight. The
more that couples can follow these rules, the more likely it is
that they can have open communication while maintaining trust
and security in the relationship:

- Before you begin, ask yourself why you feel upset. I often
  hear couples talk about how they argue over nothing.
  While the issue that triggers an argument may be triv-
  ial, often there is an underlying concern that should be
  addressed openly between the couple. For example, are
  you truly angry because your partner left crumbs on the
  counter? Or are you upset because you feel like you're
  doing an uneven share of the housework, and the crumbs
  on the counter are just one more piece of evidence? Take
  time to think about your own feelings before starting
  an argument. Fighting over crumbs won't help if there
  is a deeper issue that is making you feel hurt or angry
  or ignored.

Have a shared goal of coming to an understanding and
perhaps compromise. There isn't always a perfect answer to an
argument. Life is just too messy for that. But if both partners
have the goal of at least understanding each other, that will go a
long way towards shaping how the discussion unrolls and help
you avoid hurting each other. If it seems no agreement is possible, do your best to come to a compromise (this will mean some
give-and-take from both sides).

- Discuss one issue at a time. If you start off an argument
  by complaining that "you never drive the kids to their

activities," don't then say "you spend too much time with your friends." Trying to resolve two problems at the same time is almost impossible. Plus, when an argument starts to get off topic, it can easily become about everything a person has ever done wrong. And since we've all done a lot wrong, opening the door to that path will just lead to hurt feelings and nothing will get resolved. As much as possible, keep a discussion focused on just one issue. If something else comes up, take note and resolve to address it at a later time. "Let's talk now about getting the kids to their activities and talk about the time I'm spending with my friends later, OK?"

- No degrading language. Discuss the issue, not the person. It's fair to say "you spend too much money out of our shared account without talking to me" but NOT "you're such a loser, going around my back to spend our money." No put-downs, swearing, or name-calling. Degrading language is an attempt to express negative feelings while making sure your partner feels just as bad. This will just lead to more character attacks while the original issue is forgotten.

- Express your feelings with words and take responsibility for them. "I feel angry." "I feel hurt when you ignore my phone calls." "I feel scared when you yell." These are good ways to express how you feel. Starting with "I" is a good technique to help you take responsibility for your feelings. But no, you can't say whatever you want as long as it starts with "I." (It's not fair to say something like "I think you're a dog" or "I'm sorry that you don't agree with me.")

- Take turns talking. If only one person gets a chance to talk, that's a diatribe, not a discussion. So each partner has to both speak and then sit silently while they listen to the other person speak. This can be tough, but be careful not to interrupt when it's your turn to listen, even if you think your partner is saying something wrong or incorrect. If this rule is difficult to follow, try setting a timer, allowing one minute for each person to speak without interruption. Don't spend your partner's minute thinking about what you want to say. Listen!

- No yelling. Sometimes arguments are "won" by being the loudest, but the problem only gets worse.

- No stonewalling. Sometimes, the easiest way to respond to an argument is to refuse to speak, to hold all your thoughts inside. This refusal to communicate is called stonewalling. You might feel better temporarily, but the original issue will remain unresolved and your partner will feel more upset. If you absolutely cannot go on with the discussion at that moment, tell your partner you need to take a time-out so you can think about what they've said. Agree on a specific time to resume the discussion—whether that's in five minutes or tomorrow.

- Take a time-out if things get too heated. In a perfect world we would all follow these rules one hundred percent of the time, but life doesn't work like that. If an argument starts to become personal or heated, take a time-out. Agree on a time to come back and discuss the problem after everyone has cooled down—just as with stonewalling, make it specific (in an hour, tonight after the kids are in bed, tomorrow after work, or whatever).

Bringing the Hierarchy to Life Through Communication

Remember Carson (who suffered from sexual abuse as a child) and Sasha, his wife, from chapter 5? I introduced them to the concept of Maslow's Hierarchy of Needs and asked them to consider it as a springboard for developing their spiritual intimacy and connections at all levels going forward.

They really understood how the love languages, Maslow's Hierarchy, and the concepts of four areas of intimacy combined to create their desired relationship. Yet, they were concerned about the work, and the energy it would take to get here. "I mean we have kids and jobs and you want us to think about this too," Sasha exclaimed. So we broke it down with simple exercises.

COGNITIVE/EMOTIONAL EXCHANGE

Carson and Sasha were assigned to select a word from the Feelings Word Chart (introduced in chapter 1) each day. You can see an example in Figure 7.4 from a day when Carson was feeling angry, and Sasha was feeling peaceful.

Sad	Happy	Hurt	Helped	Insecure	Confident	Tired	Energized
Depressed	Hopeful	Abused	Cherished	Weak	Strong	Indifferent	Determined
Lonely	Supported	Forgotten	Befriended	Hopeless	Brave	Bored	Inspired
Disgusted	Charmed	Ignored	Appreci-ated	Doubtful	Certain	Drained	Creative
Carson: Angry	Grateful	Judged	Understood	Scared	Assured	Sick	Healthy
Frustrated	Calm	Offended	Commend-ed	Anxious	Prepared	Exhausted	Renewed
Annoyed	Amused	Victimized	Empowered	Defeated	Successful	Dull	Vibrant
Discour-aged	Optimistic	Rejected	Accepted	Worthless	Valuable	Weary	Alert
Upset	Content	Cursed	Blessed	Guilty	Forgiven	Paralyzed	Enlivened
Despairing	Joyful	Destroyed	Healed	Ugly	Beautify	Powerless	Strength-ened
Uninter-ested	Enthusi-astic	Hated	Loved	Pressured	At ease	Dejected	Motivated
Disap-pointed	Thrilled	Despised	Esteemed	Forced	Encour-aged	Listless	Focused
Hateful	Loving	Mistreated	Taken care of	Stressed	**Sasha: Peaceful**	Burned-out	Rejuve-nated
Bitter	Kind	Crushed	Reassured	Nervous	Relaxed	Fatigued	Invigorated
Sorrowful	Celebratory	Injured	Made whole	Worried	Secure	Blah	Animated
Mournful	Overjoyed	Tortured	Saved	Embar-rassed	Comforted	Stale	Refreshed

Figure 7.4: Feeling Word Chart—Carson and Sasha Example

When they did this exercise, each would spend 15 minutes, uninterrupted, talking about:

- *Why* the feeling they chose arose that day;
- Whether or not the feeling was connected to another;
- Whether or not this was a new feeling or when they had experienced it before;
- Whether or not they also noticed a sensation in their body;
- How they did or did not manage the feeling;
- How the feeling impacted the rest of the day.

The idea is to spend 30 minutes just expressing emotions without judgment to create emotional safety in the relationship. Carson and Sasha were instructed not to use "you," not to blame or criticize, and to offer an alternative to how they might use the emotion that came up positively in the future. They were excitedly cautious. If they decided to continue the conversation, it was up to them. At the end of the day, it is about gaining a deeper understanding of your mate.

By using this simple tool, Carson and Sasha found that they were able to alleviate some of the stress for each other in these conversations. For example, it turned out that on the day Carson felt angry, he talked about the difficulty he had getting lunch when he had to be in the field. He would often skip lunch, so he would be quite hungry on the drive home and hangry by the time he arrived. Not only did this impact their evenings immediately upon his arrival, but late in the day Carson was also making mistakes at work directly connected to his lack of energy. Sasha picked up on it and without deep discussion, began making him a sandwich for lunch with a snack box for the afternoon.

LUNCH BAG EXERCISE

Another exercise that Carson and Sasha did uses plain brown lunch bags. Each partner writes down five activities on separate pieces of paper that are examples of their preferred love languages in action. They put them in brown lunch bags that the partners exchange without talking about the items they wrote down. The idea is that each partner should complete the tasks from the bag they got as often as possible over a two-week period.

Carson, whose languages are words of affirmation and physical touch, wrote down:

1. Express in detail what you appreciate when I do something you like, talk about my strengths (what do I do well).

2. Tell me you love me at least four times a day.

3. Try a new sexual position from the book.

4. Encourage my cooking.

5. Hold my hand in public.

Sasha, whose primary languages are quality time and physical touch, wrote:

1. Set up a date night (even if at home).

2. Watch an entire movie with me.

3. Perform oral sex on me until we orgasm without penetration.

4. Go to bed with me.

5. Put away your phone and talk to me for 15 minutes each day (no work, kids, or money discussions).

By using this exercise, Carson and Sasha realized how much they had ignored one another in the smallest way. They needed to work on the simplest things at the base of Maslow's Hierarchy. Carson expressed that he had been frustrated because he felt he was not good enough for Sasha's high standards and thus stopped trying. "I could say more positive things to you," Sasha said, "I just did not think about it as a need because I prioritized everything else a bit higher. I'm sorry."

"Couple-Actualization"

Developing deeper intimacy takes work. Above all, we need to have opportunities that will allow us to listen (ears only) to and hear (full body experience) what our partner is saying and express ourselves in ways that foster connection rather than degrade intimacy in our relationship:

- We can listen to them to hear their hearts speak to us.
- We can adjust our lives and belief systems to accommodate them.
- We can cover their weaknesses and help them strengthen these areas.

- We can discuss with them what we expect from them and from the relationship to avoid misunderstanding.

- We can endeavor to explain our actions and decisions to them. We carry them on the journey of discovery together.

- We can encourage them to tell us their fears and not use these fears against them, and mitigate the opportunities for these fears to come true.

- We can speak words of affirmation to them.

- We can show them that we've got their back. We don't just say it; we live the promise.

- We can be willing to forgive and apologize when we have done wrong.

- We can do everything possible to ensure that we are committed to their peace and contentment.

When all these components come together, couples can reach the top level of Maslow's Hierarchy. In the typical version, that is "self-actualization." Applying his model to intimacy and focusing on better communication helps partners achieve what I think of as "couple-actualization," where the couple is able to achieve the full potential of their relationship. This is the culmination of all the intimacy we have discussed: cognitive, emotional, spiritual, and lastly physical.

Couple-actualization is the moment when you realize that your partner truly connects with you across multiple levels of intimacy. I say multiple because we are working with grace and not perfection. It is possible to maneuver up and down the hierarchy in various ways as you get used to how these ideals work for your relationship. This principle will help your partner know how to touch you sexually in ways that make you feel loved and recognize what brings you immense pleasure outside the bedroom. Your partner will come to understand what you need to feel safe so you can be more open and more vulnerable. You will be able to build a healthy vibrant relationship on your own terms. Trust each other as you work the process. Remember, "faith without works is dead" (James 2:17). The same can be said of relationships and marriage!

CONCLUSION

Beginning the Journey to Into-Me-See

I have spent more than 20 years as a therapist and relationship coach helping couples understand intimacy and how mental health influences relationships. Every time I meet with a couple for the first time, I let them know that they are not in the room alone. All the people who are a part of their life experience enter the room with them. Often, we will have to weed through that history to find the path they choose to take.

I'll admit there is some risk to opening the Pandora's box of personal history. It might initially appear that there is no hope for happiness. Couples may see that their relationship is at an all-time low. But the questions I get them to think about can also be a positive catalyst; it opens the door for a dialogue the couple has never had before about what each person wants from the relationship.

I assure them that improving intimacy is not a 24-hour/7-day-a-week job. What it requires is taking advantage of moments that create opportunities for increased connection. It is these moments that give life to intimacy in every romantic relationship. And yes, we all know that life would be simpler if intimacy came easily. If we could quickly peer into our partner's emotions and experiences and understand their desires and motivations. If we knew exactly what to say or do in any situation to provide everything from comfort to affirmation to arousal.

Unfortunately, as we've talked about in this book, intimacy is seldom simple or easy. That is especially true for Black couples who are dealing with negative cultural influences and experiences that hinder the growth of intimacy in their relationships. Some of these hindrances are generational, others environmental, and many others are created in our thoughts, generating emotional instability.

As a result of these challenges, Black couples are bombarded with age-old narratives that can be detrimental to their union. They struggle to cast away the negative effects of learned behaviors, experiences, and instructions. They become mired in loveless and visionless relationships.

But what I hope I've made clear in the book is that true intimacy can be achieved by couples who are willing to put in the work and maintain the change. When Black couples can remove the garment of inherited fear, prejudices, and animosity within themselves and unlearn negative teachings, they can achieve a higher level of intimacy than they ever imagined.

Many people have hurt their spouses because they did not understand what it takes to be intimate with their partner and what their partner was trying to teach them by pursuing Into-Me-See. If couples will make a committed and conscious effort to become better lovers, they will have a relationship that is not based on obligation, but intimacy. By doing this, partners can heal each other's wounds and repair their broken skin.

Intimacy allows us to be authentic in our individuality and embrace our differences in our coupling. It allows us to use our understanding of self to love our partner unconditionally. Throughout the book, I've provided a number of practical steps you can take to shed old patterns of behavior. Here are a few last principles that will help you succeed as you move towards Into-Me-See:

- Recognize every encounter with your partner as an opportunity to create intimate memories. Focus your attention on your partner when you are together. Don't let the distractions of everyday life send a message that you don't care or aren't interested in them.

- Become more reliable in meeting your partner's needs when you are truly able to do so. Intimacy requires consistency. It is not possible to meet every need (for example, your partner's need for a parent's love cannot be met by you). However, if it is in your power to meet the expectations of a need, be consistent.

- Remember, "I love you" can be expressed in different ways. It might be verbalized in "call me when you arrive at your destination," "do you want a cup of coffee?," "I enjoy being with you," or even "want to watch a movie together?" The sentiment might be expressed when your partner sweeps the floor, does the laundry, or takes you away for a romantic weekend. Do not dismiss these moments of connection just because you did not hear it as the words "I love you."

- Practice being authentic and vulnerable with your partner. I've talked a lot about the need for reciprocity, where partners are equally vulnerable and sharing when it comes to intimacy. If only one person is vulnerable, you can't have intimacy. Have the courage to be open with your partner about your true feelings and thoughts. If your partner has opened their heart and become vulnerable, match the level of vulnerability. Protect the interest of your partner because of their expressed vulnerability.

- Really listen; suspend judgment. Ask questions, wait and listen for an explanation, and then endeavor to understand your partner's ideas and desires. Silence the voice that would respond with criticism or derision. Seek to affirm and recognize your partner's viewpoint, allowing your partner room to express themselves freely. Giving your partner the freedom to be expressive is a show of respect. The goal is understanding one another's opinions and perspectives—*not* agreeing on everything. It is okay not to agree in some areas.

- Commit to the journey of experiencing all four aspects of intimacy with your partner. Talk about your past and ideas about what's happening in the world, your community, and your family (cognitive intimacy). Build a broader vocabulary around the full range of feelings that are influencing your behavior (emotional intimacy). Express your desires for touching and physical connection (physical intimacy). Talk about your core beliefs and values (spiritual intimacy).

- Be kind to each other by filling each other with words of affirmation. Acknowledge your partner's presence, praise them for achievements large and small, support them as they pursue their own goals and aspirations. Never belittle or demean them; especially in front of others.

- Work on your individual mental health. Feeling irritable and overwhelmed when your partner is busy, having difficulty verbalizing your needs, or believing that you and your partner must do and love the same things are some of the signs of tremendous anxiety. It's very difficult to achieve intimacy when you are anxious or depressed. As I've discussed, bringing mental health concerns into the open is particularly challenging in the Black community. But it is critical to identify and deal with any mental health issues that are preventing you from achieving the intimacy you seek.

- Seek professional help. The changes talked about in this book are seldom quick or easy, and the actions needed to make those changes aren't always clear. There are many options available, such as meeting with a licensed mental health professional, marriage and family therapist, psychologist, psychiatrist, licensed professional social worker, counselor, or meeting with a support group. They can help you figure out what issues are affecting your relationship (including any mental health concerns) and identify simple steps you can take as a couple to slowly build the relationship and intimacy you want.

Tools for Turning Goals into Action

Feeling Words Chart

The purpose of this chart is to help couples improve their ability to express emotions. One way to use this chart is to provide the basis for a discussion about emotions. In the example from chapter 5:

- Carson and Sasha each circled the word that described what they were feeling.

- They would then each spend 15 uninterrupted minutes (for a total of 30 minutes) talking about:

    - *Why* the feeling they chose arose that day;

    - Whether or not the feeling was connected to another;

    - Whether or not this was a new feeling or when they had experienced it before;

    - Whether or not they also noticed a sensation in their body;

    - How they did or did not manage the feeling;

    - How the feeling impacted the rest of the day.

APPENDIX TOOL 1: FEELINGS WORD CHART

Sad	Happy	Hurt	Helped	Insecure	Confident	Tired	Energized
Depressed	Hopeful	Abused	Cherished	Weak	Strong	Indifferent	Determined
Lonely	Supported	Forgotten	Befriended	Hopeless	Brave	Bored	Inspired
Disgusted	Charmed	Ignored	Appreci-ated	Doubtful	Certain	Drained	Creative
Angry	Grateful	Judged	Understood	Scared	Assured	Sick	Healthy
Frustrated	Calm	Offended	Commend-ed	Anxious	Prepared	Exhausted	Renewed
Annoyed	Amused	Victimized	Empowered	Defeated	Successful	Dull	Vibrant
Discour-aged	Optimistic	Rejected	Accepted	Worthless	Valuable	Weary	Alert
Upset	Content	Cursed	Blessed	Guilty	Forgiven	Paralyzed	Enlivened
Despairing	Joyful	Destroyed	Healed	Ugly	Beautify	Powerless	Strength-ened
Uninter-ested	Enthusi-astic	Hated	Loved	Pressured	At ease	Dejected	Motivated
Disap-pointed	Thrilled	Despised	Esteemed	Forced	Encour-aged	Listless	Focused
Hateful	Loving	Mistreated	Taken care of	Stressed	Peaceful	Burned-out	Rejuve-nated
Bitter	Kind	Crushed	Reassured	Nervous	Relaxed	Fatigued	Invigorated
Sorrowful	Celebratory	Injured	Made whole	Worried	Secure	Blah	Animated
Mournful	Overjoyed	Tortured	Saved	Embar-rassed	Comforted	Stale	Refreshed

TOOL 2

Words of Affirmation

EXAMPLE AFFIRMATIONS

1. I am so proud of who you are.

2. Thank you for loving me, even when I'm not that lovable.

3. I love you more today than any day before.

4. I can't wait to experience the rest of life with you.

5. Your decisions, hard work, and loving heart make me so proud to be your partner.

6. You understand me more than anyone. I can't believe how lucky I am to have you.

7. I can't wait till you get home from work!

8. I missed you so much today!

9. How can I make you feel more loved?

10. How can I try to understand you better?

11. I'm praying for you today. You've got this!

12. I feel so safe with your protection.

13. I will always respect and honor you.

14. I can't wait to tell my friends how you helped me!

15. You provide so much for us.

16. Your arms are the only place I want to be.

17. You can always make me laugh. I'm so happy I have you!

18. You can trust me.

19. If that's where you want to lead us, I will follow your decision.

20. I love knowing that you want me.

21. I only want you.

22. I love doing projects together. Hard work and laughter is the best with you!

23. I admire your integrity and I know others do too.

24. I still have moments where I am speechlessly thankful for our marriage.

25. I know we don't always see eye to eye, but it's reassuring to know we are always on the same team.

Guidelines for Words of Affirmation

- Affirmations start with the words "I AM."

- Affirmations are positive. Never use the word "not" in an affirmation.

   - WRONG: I am not afraid of public speaking.

- RIGHT: I am confidently delivering a presentation.
- Affirmations are short.
- Affirmations are specific.
  - WRONG: I am driving a new car.
  - RIGHT: I am driving a new black Range Rover.
- Affirmations are in the present tense and use words that end in "ing."
  - I am driving a new Honda CRV.
- Affirmations have a feeling word in them.
  - I am confidently delivering a great presentation.
- Affirmations are about yourself.
  - All of your affirmations should be to change your own behavior, not someone else's behavior.

Self-Affirmations Exercise

GOAL

To change negative language you use to describe yourself into positive language that will help build confidence and commitment to move forward.

Instructions:

1. Review the example affirmations and guidelines for affirmations (Tool 2, p. 143).

2. Write your example statements of affirmation using the space below. Be sure to follow the guidelines.

3. Then use the instructions on "How to Use Self-Esteem Affirmations" (p. 148) to do the exercise.

WRITING YOUR OWN VERSION

Now that you understand the pattern for creating an affirmation, use the space below to write your own affirmations that you can use for yourself (not your partner).

MY AFFIRMATIONS

_____

_____

_____

_____

_____

_____

_____

_____

_____

_____

_____

_____

_____

HOW TO USE SELF-ESTEEM AFFIRMATIONS (POSITIVE SELF-TALK)

- Set big goals and stay mindful of your goals (write them and place them somewhere you can see them every day).

- Say and visualize your affirmations every day.

- Take time to see yourself accomplishing the goals you've set.

- Think about how good it will feel once you have accomplished your goals—feel what you'll feel when the goal is accomplished.

- Here's an example of how you'd use all the steps listed above:

Imagine your goal was to become a professional singer, but you've always told yourself you couldn't do it because you didn't believe in yourself enough. Here is how you would use the self-esteem affirmations exercise in four steps:

1. Change your self-talk to sound like the following:
   - I have a great voice.
   - I am an excellent performer; I am a wonderful singer.

2. Give your dream or goal a deadline like the following example:
   - I will have a song in the top 10 of the music charts two years from today.

3. Create an affirmation like the following:
   - I am happily listening to the radio and hear that my song has reached the top 10.

4. Visualize yourself having achieved your goal.

TIPS

- Do the visualization every day for at least three minutes three times a day:
  - When you wake up,
  - At lunch,
  - Before you go to bed.
- Sit down in a quiet place, get relaxed, and begin to play the movie in your mind's eye.
  - Our example person would envision themselves as a successful chart-topping singer, singing on stage with their band and backup singers. They would see the dancers and the crowd that has come to see them perform. They would try to hear the music, hear the sounds coming from the crowd because they are enjoying their performance.
- Do this regularly and you will begin to see amazing results in your life.

The reason this works is that when you say your affirmations and play your success movie in your mind's eye every day, it makes something happen to your brain. Your brain begins to subconsciously look for ways to make what you have been saying and seeing happen. You begin to see opportunities you hadn't seen before. You begin to eliminate the beliefs that have held you back and made you doubt yourself, and you begin to take action towards the fulfillment of your goals. That's the power of affirmation.

Identifying Your Love Language

Below is a recap of the five love languages adapted from the work of Dr. Gary Chapman. Review the descriptions, then use the quiz (p. 155) below to help identify your primary love language(s). There is a tally sheet (p. 158) to help you interpret the results.

1. **Words of Affirmation**

   - Actions don't always speak louder than words. If this is your love language, unsolicited compliments mean the world to you. Hearing the words "I love you" is important. Hearing the reasons behind that love sends your spirits skyward. Insults can leave you shattered and are not easily forgotten.

2. **Quality Time**

   - For those whose love language is spoken with quality time, nothing says "I love you" like full, undivided attention. Being there for this type of person is critical, but really being there—with the TV off, fork and knife down, and all chores and tasks on standby—makes your significant other feel truly special and loved. Distractions, postponed dates, or the failure to listen can be especially hurtful.

3. **Receiving Gifts**

   - Don't mistake this love language for materialism; the receiver of gifts thrives on the love, thoughtfulness, and effort behind the gift. If you speak this language, the perfect gift or gesture shows that you are known, you are cared for, and you are prized above whatever was sacrificed to bring the gift to you. A missed birthday, anniversary, or a hasty, thoughtless gift would be disastrous—so would the absence of everyday gestures.

4. **Acts of Service**

   - Can vacuuming the floors really be an expression of love? Absolutely! Anything you do to ease the burden of responsibilities weighing on an acts of service person will speak volumes. The words he or she most want to hear: "Let me do that for you." Laziness, broken commitments, and making more work for them tell speakers of this language their feelings don't matter.

5. **Physical Touch**

   - This language isn't all about the bedroom. A person whose primary language is physical touch is, not surprisingly, very touchy. Hugs, pats on the back, holding hands, and thoughtful touches on the arm, shoulder, or face—they can all be ways to show excitement, concern, care, and love. Physical presence and accessibility are crucial, while neglect or abuse can be unforgivable and destructive.

The Five Love Languages Quiz

I n each pair of words, select the one you prefer most of your two options, the one that fits the best right now. Circle the letter to the right of the option you most prefer. Following the quiz, you'll find a tally sheet to help you interpret the results.

1	I like to receive notes of affirmation.	A
	I like to be hugged.	E
2	I like to spend one-to-one time with a person who is special to me.	B
	I feel loved when someone gives practical help to me.	D
3	I like it when people give me gifts.	C
	I like leisurely visits with friends and loved ones.	B
4	I feel loved when people do things to help me.	D
	I feel loved when people touch me.	E
5	I feel loved when someone I love or admire puts his or her arm around me.	E
	I feel loved when I receive a gift from someone I love or admire.	C
6	I like to go places with friends and loved ones.	B
	I like to high-five or hold hands with people who are special to me.	E

continued

7	Visible symbols of love (gifts) are very important to me.	C
	I feel loved when people affirm me.	E
8	I like to sit close to people whom I enjoy being around.	E
	I like for people to tell me I am beautiful/handsome.	A
9	I like to spend time with friends and loved ones.	B
	I like to receive little gifts from friends and loved ones.	C
10	Words of acceptance are important to me.	A
	I know someone loves me when they help me.	D
11	I like being together and doing things with friends and loved ones.	B
	I like it when kind words are spoken to me.	A
12	What someone does affects me more than what they say.	D
	Hugs make me feel connected and valued.	E
13	I value praise and try to avoid criticism.	A
	Several small gifts mean more to me than one large gift.	C
14	I feel close to someone when we are talking or doing something together.	B
	I feel closer to friends and loved ones when they touch me often.	E
15	I like for people to compliment my achievements.	A
	I know people love me when they do things for me that they don't enjoy doing.	D
16	I like to be touched as friends and loved ones walk by.	E
	I like it when people listen to me and show genuine interest in what I am saying.	B
17	I feel loved when friends and loved ones help me with jobs or projects.	D
	I really enjoy receiving gifts from friends and loved ones.	C
18	I like for people to compliment my appearance.	A
	I feel loved when people take time to understand my feelings.	B

19	I feel secure when a special person is touching me.	E
	Acts of service make me feel loved.	D
20	I appreciate the many things that special people do for me.	D
	I like receiving gifts that special people make for me.	C
21	I really enjoy the feeling I get when someone gives me undivided attention.	B
	I really enjoy the feeling I get when someone helps me make decisions.	D
22	I feel loved when a person celebrates my birthday with a gift.	C
	I feel loved when a person celebrates my birthday with meaningful words.	A
23	I know a person is thinking of me when he or she gives me a gift.	C
	I feel loved when a person helps with my chores.	D
24	I appreciate it when someone listens patiently and doesn't interrupt me.	B
	I appreciate it when someone remembers special days with a gift.	C
25	I like knowing loved ones are concerned enough to help with my daily tasks.	D
	I enjoy extended trips with someone who is special to me.	B
26	I enjoy kissing or being kissed by people with whom I am close.	E
	I enjoy receiving a gift given for no special reason.	C
27	I like to be told that I am appreciated.	A
	I like for a person to look at me when we are talking.	B
28	Gifts from a friend or loved one are always special to me.	C
	I feel good when a friend or loved one touches me.	E
29	I feel loved when a person enthusiastically does some task I have requested.	D
	I feel loved when I am told how much I am needed.	A
30	I need to be touched every day.	E
	I need words of encouragement daily.	A

Tally the Results

Count up the number of answers in each category (A, B, C, D, and E).

	A	B	C	D	E
Total Count					

Check the box under the category with the highest count total. That is your primary love language.

☐ A = Words of Affirmation

☐ B = Quality Time

☐ C = Receiving Gifts

☐ D = Acts of Service

☐ E = Physical Touch

To take the quiz online, go to www.5lovelanguages.com/assessment.

Spouse Satisfaction Survey

Spouse Satisfaction Survey

The tables below and on the next page constitute the satisfaction survey referenced in chapter 1. I use this survey to help couples establish a baseline of where their relationship is now and what areas need the most work in order to increase satisfaction.

PART 1: ASSURANCE AND SECURITY

The purpose of this questionnaire is to provide your spouse feedback on your perspective of the level of assurance and security in the relationship. This questionnaire intends to identify areas for improvement. Please read each statement below and score each from 0 to 10. Then calculate each number at the end. Best results are experienced when you are authentic in your response. This questionnaire should not be employed to degrade or humiliate but to establish a baseline so you can build a road map toward discovering your unique, intimate expressions.

Please read carefully and evaluate each sentence.	0-10
1	I feel assured that my spouse/partner loves and appreciates my company. I feel emotionally connected with my spouse/partner.	
2	I feel assured that my spouse/partner loves my body, shape, size, taste, and smell. Their enthusiasm about my presence makes me feel proud to have them in my life.	
3	My spouse/partner is dedicated to pleasing me sexually and fulfills my sexual needs.	
4	My spouse/partner loves me and is sensitive to the needs of my vagina, vulva, and uterus (yoni) or penis, scrotum, and perineum (lingam).	
5	When spending quality time, I can sense that my spouse/partner wants to be with me.	
6	Whenever I express a concern, my spouse/partner responds to resolving the issue and puts my mind at ease, knowing I will be taken care of. I don't have to remind them more than twice.	
7	My spouse/partner showers me with appreciation, affirmation, and often compliments me. My spouse/partner makes me feels good about myself.	
8	The level of trust and security I feel when I'm with my spouse/partner. They take care of me when we are together.	
9	My spouse/partner respects me and values my opinion. I feel that I can provide my honest thoughts without them becoming defensive.	
10	My overall satisfaction with my emotional and spiritual connection with my spouse/partner.	

Overall Score _____   **Survey Date** _____

PART 2: INTIMACY AND ROMANCE

The purpose of this questionnaire is to provide your spouse feedback on your perspective of intimacy and romance in the relationship. This questionnaire intends to identify areas for improvement. Please read each statement below and score each from 0 to 10. Then calculate each number at the end. Best results are experienced when you are authentic in your response. This questionnaire should not be employed to degrade or humiliate but to establish a baseline so you can build a road map toward discovering your unique, intimate expressions.

Please read carefully and evaluate each sentence.	0-10
1	When intimate with my spouse/partner, they attend to my sudden body changes, language, or signals.	
2	My spouse/partner's touch is gentle, compassionate, and loving. My mind, body, and soul melts in their hands.	
3	During foreplay, my spouse/partner takes his time with me instead of rushing to my genitals. My spouse/partner is not clumsy, rough, or poking.	
4	My spouse/partner assures I'm highly aroused before attempting penetration.	
5	My spouse/partner pays attention to my other needs, such as emotional, physical, mental, and spiritual.	
6	My spouse/partner is aware of my erogenous zones and frequents them when we're intimate.	
7	My spouse/partner uses words, ideas, and fantasies that turn me on.	
8	Our lovemaking is inspiring and spontaneous with novelty, excitement, and newness.	
9	My spouse/partner shows interest in my turn-ons and listens when I attempt to demonstrate others to them.	
10	My overall satisfaction with our sex life.	

Overall Score _____ Survey Date _____

Please help us with our research by going to https://www.tmicounselingandcoaching.com/take-our-surveys

All responses are anonymous and you will receive your results immediately.

About the Author

Becoming intimate or nurturing intimacy with your partner seems like it should be easy. It can be. Yet, for some people it is an arduous task that makes them feel very vulnerable. If you've ever had difficulty achieving this milestone in your relationship or thought you needed to raise your intimacy bar, I have three words for you: "You are right!" Kudos for actually acknowledging that there is a problem.

Being a licensed marriage and family therapist, I understand the intricacies of a deep, intimate exchange between two people who love, adore, and desire one another but on most days can't seem to muster the fluidity of affection to create and sustain intimate connection. I teach couples to flourish in intimate relationships. After having spent years helping couples resolve their intimacy mishaps and explore their intimacy needs, I am motivated to unveil the many untold truths regarding the myths and realities of intimacy between Black couples. Despite centuries of negative narratives about the intimacy of Black couples, I use this medium to reveal what sometimes limits a couple's desire in order to actualize healthy intimacy.

Without harboring the desire to demonize anyone, I expose unspoken truths about the challenges to healthy intimate relationships. These challenges have always been there, but because no one is willing to talk with unrelenting honesty and depths of emotion, attaining complete intimacy remains an illusion in many relationships. As James Baldwin once said, "Not everything that is faced will be changed, but nothing can be changed until it is faced." Intimacy is a desire couples are mostly unprepared to discuss, yet one they are in desperate need to live. It is oxygen to a relationship. I hope *Into-Me-See* accelerates the innate desire of Black couples toward intimacy. My aim with this book is to light the paths for couples on their journeys to discovering their unique intimate expressions.